TEAM-SPIRITED PARENTING

TEAM-SPIRITED PARENTING

8 Essential Principles for Parenting Success

Darlene Powell Hopson, Ph.D.
and
Derek S. Hopson, Ph.D.

JOHN WILEY & SONS, INC.
New York • Chichester • Weinheim • Brisbane • Singapore • Toronto

This book is printed on acid-free paper. ⊗

Copyright © 2001 by Darlene Powell Hopson, Ph.D., and Derek S. Hopson, Ph.D.
All rights reserved

Published by John Wiley & Sons, Inc.
Published simultaneously in Canada

Design and production by Navta Associates, Inc.

No part of this publication may be reproduced, stored in a retrieval system, or transmitted
in any form or by any means, electronic, mechanical, photocopying, recording, scanning,
or otherwise, except as permitted under Section 107 or 108 of the 1976 United States
Copyright Act, without either the prior written permission of the Publisher, or authoriza-
tion through payment of the appropriate per-copy fee to the Copyright Clearance Center,
222 Rosewood Drive, Danvers, MA 01923, (978) 750-8400, fax (978) 750-4744. Requests
to the Publisher for permission should be addressed to the Permissions Department, John
Wiley & Sons, Inc., 605 Third Avenue, New York, NY 10158-0012, (212) 850-6011, fax
(212) 850-6008, e-mail: PERMREQ@WILEY.COM.

This publication is designed to provide accurate and authoritative information in regard
to the subject matter covered. It is sold with the understanding that the publisher is not
engaged in rendering professional services. If professional advice or other expert assistance
is required, the services of a competent professional person should be sought.

Library of Congress Cataloging-in-Publication Data
Hopson, Darlene Powell.
    Team-spirited parenting : 8 essential principles for parenting success / by Darlene
Powell Hopson and Derek S. Hopson.
        p. cm.
    Includes bibliographical references and index.
    ISBN 0-471-34569-5 (cloth : alk. paper)
        1. Parenting. 2. Parent and child. 3. Communication in the family.
I. Hopson, Derek S. II. Title.

HQ755.8 .H66 2001
649'.1—dc21   00-51369

Printed in the United States of America

This book is dedicated to our wonderful children, Dotteanna and Derek Jr. You are truly our greatest gifts in life and blessings from God. As your parents, we have learned to love more deeply than words could ever express and the mind could ever imagine.

Contents

Preface

Becoming a Team-Spirited Parent

Helping parents become team-spirited is our passion, both as clinical psychologists and as spiritual beings. Over the past fifteen years we have built up our private practice at the Hopson Center for Psychological and Educational Services. As a husband-and-wife team, we've conducted hundreds of workshops. Along the way we've written five books, contributed to Disney Online, and served on the advisory board of *Child* magazine.

The number of people we have counseled keeps growing dramatically, because millions of families need what we have to offer: down-to-earth, practical principles and techniques that have the potential to turn a parent's loneliness and frustration into joy.

Sara, for example, is typical of the people we have helped to change their lives through team-spirited principles. When Sara came to us for counseling recently, she was looking specifically for help with a problem she had identified in her son Jared's behavior. She had feelings of anger and resentment toward Jared's father, Frank, who was not as involved as she was in Jared's life.

Over the next few months we helped Sara create a team spirit in the family—starting with renewing her own spirit, then reaching out to Frank. As their mutual understanding of the value and purpose of team-spirited parenting grew, Frank and Sara got more constructively involved in directing Jared's behavior. As their parenting skills increased, they became more confident. They learned how to create a feeling of cooperation, support, and mutual respect in their home. As a family, they began to share more of the pleasures of life, too. Even though it was hard for Sara and Frank at first, they each grew more comfortable with sharing their concerns about Jared with family, friends, teachers, and their pastor.

To Sara's surprise, it was sometimes as hard to share the credit for Jared's accomplishments as it was to share his problems and frustrations. But eventually she accepted the fact that trying to parent alone had become almost overwhelming for her and was not helping her son.

She could have clung to Jared's problems and been left with a sad sense of "what if?" She could have refused to make the effort to try the fresh approach of building a team for support. But she didn't. Instead, she took the leap of faith to try something new, with our guidance.

Now Sara has the type of parenting partnership we believe you are seeking. Most important, by parenting in a team-spirited manner, she has seen miraculous changes occur in Jared's behavior.

Having been married for fifteen years ourselves, we understand Frank and Sara's victory. We are the parents of two children, a thirteen-year-old daughter and an eight-year-old son. We've also had the chance to parent children of extended family members who lived with us for periods of time. Our twenty-two-year-old nephew is attending a nearby college now, and we continue to use a team approach in guiding him. Actually, there are few parenting experiences we haven't had, from the nearly devastating to the absolutely wonderful—and just about everything in between. So we can appreciate that working together to be better parents requires persistent and determined effort. But parenting is a lot of work, anyway, so it makes sense to try to improve as parents even without a crisis to solve. Indeed, we find that the better parents we become, the harder we want to work at it. We are always striving to raise our standards to an even higher level. And the higher the level, the greater the rewards have been for our children, and the more satisfying the journey has been for us.

Are You Ready to Catch the Spirit?

From professional and personal experience, we can usually identify that point when a parent is really motivated to try team-spirited principles. Are you ready? Answering the following questions will help you find out:

Are you willing to examine your past relationships to your own parents, your children, and your parenting partner? Most parents entered parenthood with great hopes, expectations, and aspirations. They love their children with a passion that can sometimes feel more intense than romance. But parenting is a tricky business, and problems are inevitable. When team-spirited parents feel angry, disappointed, or frustrated with themselves, their partner, or their children, they are not afraid of looking inside themselves for reasons, clues, and possible solutions.

Are you committed to being as involved with your child as your child needs for you to be? Team-spirited parents understand that parenting requires time, even when it is in short supply. To become fully involved, they are prepared not only to give their children time on request but to volunteer time, offering it willingly.

Are you willing, when necessary, to sacrifice for your children? Team-spirited parents are willing to accept that in most cases their children's needs are a higher priority than their own. Sometimes this means inconveniencing themselves in order to be there for a son or daughter. This prospect does not trouble them, because they can imagine sometimes putting aside their own interests, activities, and ambitions to meet the true needs of a child.

Do you wish you could communicate more effectively with your parenting partner and your child? Team-spirited parents soon figure out that communicating means not only talking but also listening actively. If listening more often is the price they have to pay to develop more open, nurturing relationships with their children, they are willing to pay the price.

Are you prepared to share joy as well as responsibility? Team-spirited parents welcome each new day as another chance to improve their game. They understand that having fun along the way nourishes and replenishes the spirit.

If you answered "yes" every time, or even "I think so," then you have come to the right book. Join our team through these pages. Important information, specific answers, clarifying questions, and powerful examples lie ahead, and a more soul-satisfying, successful parenting experience awaits you.

Acknowledgments

First and foremost, thanks to Almighty God for guidance and inspiration. Thank you to our spirited team, including our parents, family, extended family, and friends, for supporting us in applying the 8 Essential Principles for Parenting Success in our daily lives.

We have had a phenomenal editor, albeit a demanding one. She consistently raised the bar. Carole Hall expected and accepted only excellence. She inspired and motivated us to extend and enhance our work. Carole was able to perceive and believe in our capability to write this book. We thank her and we love her. We also thank Wiley managing editor Kimberly Monroe and our copy editor, Maureen Sugden.

Tom Clavin assisted in developing the foundation of the book, and we are grateful for his contribution. Liza Burby worked effectively as a team player, skillfully expanding on Tom's contribution and completing the final draft. Without our agent, Nat Sobel, persistently advising and supporting as dedicated agents do, we would not have had this wonderful opportunity, and we are very thankful to him.

TEAM-SPIRITED PARENTING

1

Make Peace with the Past: The First Principle

*I feel peace and acceptance in knowing that
the past does not control me. Every day
I have a new opportunity to relate more
lovingly to my children and my family.*

What Every Good Parent Wants

Imagine how joyful the world would be if all caring parents got what they hoped for: an emotionally healthy family in which each member relates lovingly—or at least responsibly—to the others. This is the essence of parenting success—what we all want and what we go through the ups and downs of daily living to achieve.

Everyone longs to experience the love and fulfillment of positive family life. But most parents discover that success and happiness are elusive goals. No game book clearly spells out the rules of play. Most parents are winging it, responding to crises as they come along, without expert guidance or training. Although caring deeply about one another, parents don't

1

naturally pull for each other, either. And despite wanting badly to feel connected to their children, parents aren't always there for their children when their children need them most.

Unlike sports teams, if parents and children suffer a loss, it's not just a statistic for the record books. It's an injury to the soul.

If this struggle sounds familiar to you, you are not alone. In our work as clinical psychologists and in our seminars, we've talked to hundreds of good-hearted parents who feel uneasy. They've worked hard to solve their children's problems, but the results have been uneven. They've tried to establish a positive bond with each other. But instead of a partnership, what they have formed is, at best, a fragile, temporary alliance. Frequently in conflict, they seem to be coming apart instead of coming together as a team.

But the beauty of parenting is that even when you think you've lost the game, the game goes on. And the score is never final if you are working to renew the spirit within your family. It may be true that the spirit is hidden from sight and seems lost for good, but where there's love, the spirit never dies. The important thing is that you recognize its value and believe you can bring it back.

Take a moment to answer these fifteen questions. They will help you assess the issues affecting the success of your family life. Answer *Always, Often, Rarely,* or *Never.*

1. Problems from my childhood sometimes interfere with my parenting.
2. I feel that my authority is undermined when my child's other parent disagrees with me.
3. My child's other parent and I argue about parenting.
4. I invite communication with my child's other parent.

5. Even when I'm unsure of how to deal with a problem, I know that with our faith, we'll be able to work things out as a family.

6. I allow community involvement to be a part of my parenting.

7. I am involved in my children's school- and homework.

8. I am comfortable disciplining my children.

9. I have to prod and push my children to meet their responsibilities.

10. I trust my children to support each other.

11. My children are willing to hear my opinions about their friends.

12. My children respect my point of view even when they see things differently.

13. My children and I enjoy spending time in leisure activities together.

14. I feel overwhelmed with parenting responsibilities.

15. I tend to rush my child from one commitment or activity to another.

Now add up your scores. The scoring for statements 4, 5, 6, 7, 8, 10, 11, 12, and 13 is:

Always = 4 points
Often = 3 points
Rarely = 2 points
Never = 1 point

The scoring for statements 1, 2, 3, 9, 14, and 15 is:

Always = 1 point
Often = 2 points
Rarely = 3 points
Never = 4 points

The optimal score is 60. Keeping this in mind, any score over 45 suggests that you're already functioning as a team-spirited parent. You have solid overall parenting skills and tend to focus effectively on the areas in which you'd like to do better. The techniques and ideas in this book will build your confidence and expand your knowledge.

If your score is between 25 and 45, you're aware of how difficult parenting is for you. You try hard but probably have trouble being consistent. As we help you build up your team spirit, we will be helping you learn and practice fundamental parenting skills.

The lowest possible score is 15, but anything below 25 is cause for some worry. There is a critical need for team spirit in your family. You may already be struggling with parenting problems that, left unresolved, could turn into heartbreaking situations.

Whatever amount of team spirit exists between you and your parenting partner today, the future can still be bright for your child. The point is not to worry about what you're doing wrong but to start recognizing signs of hope in what you're doing right. Parenting is a fluid process. You're always learning, simply by virtue of the fact that your children are learning. The spirit of learning is at the heart of team spirit. Your capacity to learn is what makes hope a reality. Sometimes you'll handle a dilemma in just the right way. Other times you'll get it wrong. You'd be superhuman if you didn't sometimes make mistakes.

No matter how you feel about your parenting right now, each day brings you a new opportunity to succeed. Besides, we're here to help you, and we believe that whatever healthy objectives you have for your family can be achieved.

So what could be getting in the way of the positive growth and change you want? Obviously, there are many factors to consider, starting with major behavior patterns that are rooted in your childhood. The rest of this chapter offers steps to help you assess them. Ask yourself: Could any of these issues be blocking the spirit within me, making it harder for me to keep team spirit alive?

Step One: Connect to the Power of Your Memories

Are memories controlling your life? The fact is, the most direct influence on the way you behave as a parent is the team of adults that parented you, regardless of their genetic bond to you. From small day-to-day acts to major decisions, the views that motivate your own parenting behavior are connected to the words and actions of your parents. Consciously and unconsciously, every day of your childhood you deduced what parenting was all about by watching and being affected by the people who took on those roles in your life. As children and young adults, we all assimilate, emulate, and—amazingly—even adopt the gestures and tone of voice our caretakers use. You have only to watch an infant mimic your facial gestures to understand how early in our lives this occurs.

Have you ever said to yourself, "I'm turning into my mother" or "That's just what my father used to say"? This can be reassuring if you find yourself emulating the positive behavior of one or both of your parents. It can be disconcerting if the behavior is one you recall as being confusing or in other ways painful. The challenge is to think about what effect this remembered behavior might be having on your child.

For example, if your parents were overcontrolling and fearful, you would have felt restricted as a child, unable to make your own decisions or to participate in the activities of your peers. As an adult, you might still struggle with an inability to be decisive and to take risks. When you become a parent:

- You may make a conscious effort to treat your child differently and succeed.

- You may recognize that you're continuing a negative pattern, though you do realize that you're unsatisfied with your child's behavior and are at a loss as to what to do about it.

- You may be caught in an internal struggle to push your child toward independence without really feeling comfortable doing so.

In any case, the voices you remember from your family of origin are certainly still very much present and embedded in your parenting experience. How loud they are depends on how deeply they affected you, whether you recognize their influence or not.

Think back to when you were a child and try to remember when you felt loved, secure, and valued. Can you remember being cuddled while you were read to, holding hands while shopping, and being made to feel very special on your birthday?

Now think of when you felt alone, insecure, afraid, or devalued. Can you remember being spanked, yelled at, or ridiculed?

What were your caretakers' or parents' words and actions on those occasions? How do those memories make you feel?

Step Two: Sort Out Your Issues

When an issue from your childhood carries over into your adult life, we call that a "family of origin issue." It's a broad enough term to include issues and events that had an impact on your extended family. Most likely what role these issues play will not be readily apparent to you until something happens in your own life as an impetus to self-examination. We found this to be especially true for our client Leigh.

Leigh had a good relationship with her parents and admired them as people. Her mother had worked hard to raise four children and to treat all of them equally and lovingly. Her father was a kind and considerate man who also worked very hard to support his family and save up so that his children could go to college and enter professions he didn't have the education to strive for. Sadly, he was unsuccessful in this, because when he was in his late thirties he suffered a severe injury. Leigh was only ten when the family's income was reduced to a combination of disability payments and money from the occasional cleaning jobs Leigh's mother could find. It wasn't too long before their savings dried up.

But Leigh thought this was all behind her when she came to us for counseling a couple of years ago. She is now married and has two young children. While her children were in first and third grades, she worked part-time by choice, because her husband, Mike, had his own successful business and the family was financially secure.

When her children were younger, it seemed to Leigh that she was just being sensible about not wanting to shower them with gifts at holidays and birthdays. She'd tell herself that reasonable parents don't want to raise children who will be spoiled and unappreciative. Leigh thought she was being frugal when she set some rather strict limits on presents given to her children. She said there was no guarantee that Mike's business would always be profitable, and extra money should be put aside for the future, not frittered away on toys and games.

Soon Leigh's increasing insistence on denying her children gifts, even ones from family members, became a source of tension between her and Mike. They fought constantly. Additionally, Leigh's attitude disappointed and confused her children as they heard and saw what gifts classmates received. They were upset by their parents' arguments and by what they perceived as their mother's lack of understanding of their needs. This led to discipline issues between them and their mother. It was because of this family strife that Leigh finally agreed to go to counseling.

Leigh did not immediately see a connection between her feelings and reactions to her husband and children and what she had experienced as a young girl. As she spoke about her parents, it became clear to us that Leigh and her siblings had experienced several years of severe financial hardship that had made her fear for the future—her own and that of her family. Gifts of clothing and toys were few and far between and were often hand-me-downs. Keeping a roof over their heads and putting food on their table was a continuous struggle for the family. When she was old enough, Leigh found jobs to help support the household, and she put herself through a community college.

Obviously, Leigh's unhappy and fearful feelings as a child and teenager were still part of her as a parent. Deep down she was scared that whatever financial security she and Mike had attained could be snatched away in an instant. Her way to guard against disaster was to spend money only on necessities and save the rest. Her cushion could never be secure enough. And though Leigh was a committed, loving mother, there was also some unconscious resentment toward her children because of the comparative "riches" available to them on special occasions, when Leigh as a youngster had been repeatedly denied.

The parenting problem Leigh was having was not directly related to her parents. Her family had become mired in unfortunate circumstances, but her parents had remained loving and supportive. The impact of those circumstances, including the pain of poverty and the fear of the future, was a family of origin issue. The family didn't want these circumstances, didn't deliberately cause them, and tried to cope with them as best they could. Yet for Leigh, they were impossible to ignore or overcome. It took counseling for her to finally make the connection, to heal herself and her new family, and to move beyond her past.

Family of origin issues can be complex to sort out. They may be numerous, or there may be just one overriding issue that you can't seem to get past despite sincere efforts. Perhaps it's that your father had no time for you. Or your mom was always critical. In any case, the lingering effects can be damaging to your personal emotional health and to your relationships with your children as well as with your partner. That's why it's so important that family of origin issues be recognized, acknowledged, and examined. To repress, ignore, or consciously suppress or downplay them is to deny yourself the opportunity to grow as a person and as a parent.

Step Three: Look for Positives

Don't let your past paralyze you or shake your confidence. Remember that even though our parents are our single greatest influence, they're not our only one. We're influenced also by a kindly neighbor, a dynamic teacher, an inspirational church leader, a supportive first boss, and anyone else in our lives whom we view as a mentor. Further, how we absorb our family of origin issues varies with our temperament and even our birth position. Some of us are not easily influenced by others' behavior, even that of our parents. Some of us, because of our birth order, may have had more interactions with our parents compared with younger siblings who had older siblings as buffers. All of this is to say that despite your past, you can positively influence your child. But the first step toward that positive influence is acknowledging that past and beginning to examine more carefully how it affected who you are. It's important to bring forward the positives even from a negative family of origin experience. Try to avoid unproductive feelings of resentment and bitterness.

There's power in observing your past, modifying its impact on you, and reframing it into positive lessons that can enhance your parenting style.

Perhaps those lessons will inspire you to retain at least a few of your original family traditions. Striving to be similar to your parents in terms of positives will provide your children with a sense of family legacies and traditions. Sharing positive stories and experiences, however few they may be, will give your children a sense of belonging and connection.

Step Four: Unpack the Baggage from Your Parents' Divorce

If you come from a household that experienced divorce or longtime separation, you face a unique challenge. If you haven't fully worked out feelings that were developed in childhood by that experience—if you harbor unexamined feelings of sadness, confusion, guilt, or anger—those emotions inevitably will invade your relationship with your own children. Additionally, having had your parents divorce may mean that you feel at greater risk in your relationship with your partner. It would not be surprising if you looked for "red flags" too frequently. That, too, will significantly affect your parenting. The energy that you and your partner should be drawing on together to parent your child will be diffused as you cope with your marriage.

We saw this happen to Monica and Albert.

Monica was only a teenager when her father had an affair with her best friend's mother, who also happened to be a friend of Monica's mother. Monica watched her mother endure the shock of the breakup of her marriage and the humiliation of the betrayal by her friend and husband. Perhaps unable to deal with the scene he had created, Monica's father disappeared from their lives.

The devastation to Monica's sense of trust in her father—indeed, in all her relationships with males—was one that she carried into her marriage to Albert. While this distrust caused minor conflicts for the couple before they became parents, it wasn't until their twins were born that Monica's past began to wreak havoc on their relationship.

Monica had a successful career that she enjoyed, but it was one that was often demanding of her time. Albert's job was more flexible and often allowed him to spend more time with the twins than Monica could. Monica had a hard time dealing with this, because she felt left out of the relationship. She constantly monitored Albert, questioned his time with their children, and began to set restrictions on what the twins and their father could do together. Though she couldn't identify her feelings, she was fearful that once again she was being shut out of an important relationship. The couple fought constantly, but once the twins began to cry for their father whenever their mother was alone with them, Monica realized she had a problem.

Albert insisted on therapy, and Monica reluctantly came to see us to try to salvage their marriage. Sadly, Monica was unable to get beyond the distrust issues that had affected her so deeply when her parents' marriage broke up. The couple is now divorced, and they share custody of Dale and David. We're not sure how the twins are doing, but unless Monica is willing to resolve the issues she carries from her own parents' divorce, it's almost certain that the children will grow up with unresolved issues of their own.

Had Monica perhaps had more support and guidance from her mother—and some explanation and healing from her father—she might have had some strengths on which to build a stable relationship with Albert.

Chances are that your parents' divorce has affected you in various ways. Maybe they felt so guilty about it that they overindulged you in material goods as a child, when all you really wanted from them was their reassurance that despite the demise of their relationship, they still loved you. You may believe that love is all that's necessary when it comes to your own children (which is not far off, but indulging them in a coveted toy or ice cream cone once in a while is harmless, and in fact, it's one of the joys of being a child). Or maybe because you felt deprived all around, you overindulge your own children.

Don't misunderstand us: We don't mean that if you're a child of divorce you're destined to face parenting challenges. Many divorced parents handled their situation in such a way that their children never suffered any severe or lifelong negative impact as a result. But we do mean that if you have not fully come to terms with your parents' divorce, there's a likelihood you will have to deal with it one way or another as a parent yourself. Now may be the time to sit down with your parents if you're able and have a heart-to-heart about their relationship when they were married, how they thought they handled their situation with you, and how they saw its impact on you. Their perspective might be more of an impetus to healing than you anticipate. But when you do have that heart-to-heart, blame must not be part of the process. You need to recognize that your parents did what they felt was best and coped as well as they could at the time. Your goal is to gather information to gain greater understanding for your own emotional well-being.

Step Five: Listen Carefully to the Voices on Your Message Tape

If you feel uncomfortable and guilty about delving into the past, we understand. If you loved your parents and understand that they did the best they could, you might feel guilty about even acknowledging problems, as though you're betraying them. In some ways you may even question your right to judge their parenting. After all, you're fairly new to the game yourself. These feelings are perfectly all right. A blaming attitude only makes us bitter. A healthier approach is to adopt the attitude that your parents did the best they could and that it's your responsibility to do the best you can for your own children.

What motivated, inspired, and encouraged you as a child? Was it your mother's warm embrace, your father's joyful laugh, your grandfather's supportive cheers, your aunt's praise? Whatever it was, you have internalized these experiences as an adult. If your parents praised you, you'll likely feel attached to those things. For example, my (Derek's) grandmother wouldn't allow anyone to disturb me when I was at the kitchen table studying. Not only did this simple act on her part teach me that she valued my education, it also made me feel special. The result of this one small but empowering encouragement had lasting benefits.

For your healthy development as an individual and as a parent, take a moment now to think about the past, even if it is something you feel you have no time for or you simply never think about. Below are some statements that may help jog long-forgotten childhood memories:

1. The person in my family I most identified with was
   _____.

2. I identified strongly with that person because _____.

3. Three significant attitudes that person held about parenting were _____.

4. Three significant attitudes that person held about children were _____.

5. Three significant attitudes that person held about me were _____.

6. When I was a teenager, I swore I would never do this as a parent: _____.

7. I learned most of what I know about parenting from _____.

8. The best thing my parents ever did for me was _____.

9. The worst thing my parents ever did to me was _____.

10. My parents play/don't play a large role in my parenting because _____.

Did you begin to see any patterns from your childhood that you're repeating today? Is there any issue that you feel affects your life as a parent? Did the information you remembered make you anxious or nostalgic? If it made you anxious, that's the first step toward awareness, which is critical for healing. If it made you feel warm and loved, remember this and determine how you can incorporate these actions into your own parenting style.

Step Six: Erase the Negative Messages

Your next task in sorting out the past is to erase negative messages. If you internalize negative messages, you'll surely tell yourself you can't do anything right. But if you release those messages, you can begin to accept that you can't change the past, but you can take responsibility for changing the present. Let the past inspire you to do better. Remember that you're not looking back to accuse or condemn anyone. You're looking back with compassion in order to grow. Most likely you've already begun to see that even a family history steeped in pain and bitterness can offer lessons that help us attain self-knowledge and validate our sense of worth. The more you acknowledge that past and understand the issues it has created for you, the more able you will be to transform that pain and bitterness into the power to be the parent you want to be. To help you tap into that power, we offer you a new way to interpret your past so that you can move beyond it and provide the structure and process your children depend upon.

We suggest you learn to erase the old, negative tapes of your childhood and begin anew. To do so:

1. *Listen to the tapes you're playing in your head.* What early childhood messages do you hear? Is your father saying, "You'll never amount to anything"? Is your mother whispering, "What do you have to cry about?" Darin, a client we treated, kept hearing his father's jeers about his inability to play sports as well as his father expected him to.

2. *Label the feelings you have when you hear these old tapes.* Do they make you angry? Frustrated? Sad? Resentful? How often do you replay the same messages?

3. *Examine the ways in which you've internalized old messages.* Do you berate yourself with statements like "I'll never measure up. Even my son isn't good enough"?

4. *Recognize that those old tapes might be distorted.* The adults who recorded the negative messages you hear undoubtedly carried their own psychological baggage. You don't have to take responsibility for their issues. Perhaps your father was unsuccessful in his own endeavors in life and feared that you would follow suit. You have to learn that you are not responsible for your father's disappointments.

5. *Understand that you have no control over the past.* You can't change what has already happened and shouldn't allow it to hold you captive. Continuing to lick old wounds can be an excuse to stagnate. As a parent responsible for your child's emotional and psychological development, you can't afford to be. Acknowledge the past and move on.

6. *Take responsibility for yourself in the present.* When the old tapes begin playing in your head, push the stop button. Tell yourself, "That's old business. I will no longer repeat these irrational and negative messages."

7. *Finally, rewind the tape and begin recording and playing back positive messages.* Affirm your strengths as an individual and as a parent. Tell yourself, "I am a good parent," "I can be the parent I want to be," "I am developing my parenting skills each day and I have a new opportunity to do better with my children," "I care about being there for my children."

Step Seven: Reassess Your Parenting Approach

The following chart covers six common issues: bedtime, chores, homework, literacy, anger, and peer relationships. Take a moment now to think about how you tend to approach these problems.

1. For each of these issues, check the approach in column I, II, or III that most closely reflects how you were parented.
2. Repeat the exercise, only this time check off the approach to these discipline issues that most closely reflects how you parent your children.

How Do You Approach Common Problems?

	I	II	III
1.	Demand a consistent bedtime	Identify appropriate bedtime, then enforce it	Talk and play until children get tired
2.	Insist on having the house clean	Identify appropriate chores, then assign them	Clean children's rooms and pick up after them
3.	Do step-by-step monitoring of homework	Review homework before play	Ask if homework was done or assume it has been completed
4.	Insist on having a set number of books read by a certain time	Schedule reading time for schoolwork and fun	Buy an occasional book
5.	See expression of anger as disrespect	Allow expression of anger with limits	Allow unmodulated expression of anger
6.	Insist on meeting all friends	Encourage children to invite friends over	Show little interest in meeting friends

If you checked mostly those items in column I, you may focus too much on structure with your children. You're rigid about getting things done in a certain way and by a certain time.

If you checked the majority of items in column III, you may focus too much on process, on letting your children have too much freedom without setting limits.

If you checked mostly items in column II, you have internalized a well-balanced approach to parenting. You're appropriately providing structure when your children need it most and allowing enough freedom so your children know as individuals that they matter to you.

Step Eight: Talk to Your Children about Your Past

Sometimes the way we recognize ourselves best is through our children. Have you watched your daughter struggle to accomplish something and rebuff your offers of help, then realized she's just as independent as you were? Have you watched your son handle a crowd of kids by disarming them with a joke, only to recognize he shares your sense of humor? Of course, it works the opposite way, too. Our children can learn traits we wish they hadn't.

When children ask questions about our childhood, several things are going on. One is simple curiosity. Perhaps they'll get to hear a good story. The supporting characters may include favorite aunts, uncles, or neighbors.

But more often than not, children are trying to grasp what makes you tick and gain a better understanding of who you are. At some point, usually around school age, they start to perceive their parents as fellow humans with multifaceted lives, such as people who are employees or bosses, football fans, volunteer workers, or Sunday school teachers.

Then, with so much new information to consider, children begin to compare themselves to us. They ask themselves, "Do I like the same color clothes, the same people, the same TV shows? Are my feet/hands/facial features the same? If they're different, how much? When I grow up, how much will I be like Mom and Dad?"

The bottom line for children, even though they don't initially recognize this, is that they want to know where they came from. The biological explanation is only one part of the picture. Children want to know how their parents came to be the way they are so that they can better speculate on how close they will come to matching their parents—and matching *up to* their parents. This is an inevitable—and usually constructive—part of individual development.

Are you ready, willing, and able to respond to your child's questions in an open, honest, and age-appropriate way? If so, then prepare yourself to provide answers that are truthful, informative, and constructive. Even if the story you tell isn't completely happy, your children will learn from it and draw insights about you.

Always give children just the information they ask for. Answer their questions, and don't deny what they observe with their own eyes. If you're dishonest, what they'll view as your lack of trust of them is probably far worse than whatever you could tell them truthfully about your family.

If you still have issues with your parents that your child observes—your father yells at you to shut up over Thanksgiving dinner—you have an obligation to your child to say to your father, "Please don't speak to me that way. If you persist, we'll have to leave." Whatever issues you had with your father, you have a responsibility to ensure they do not pass on to the next generation.

A final word of caution: Share experiences and information—good and bad—in ways that a child is developmentally ready to handle. You don't want to make the mistake of sharing family secrets with a child who is either likely to be merely confused by what you have to say or totally shattered.

Here's how we recommend you begin sharing the story of "you" with your child. How you do so depends on whether your child is preschool age or younger, grade school age, or an adolescent.

How to Talk to Your Preschooler

A preschooler is only beginning to develop a self-image. You need to make the visual connection to the child herself. What helps with this age group is using a photo album. Explain the basic connections between people in your family pictures and your child. For instance, did your child ever get to visit Aunt Kadija, the smiling woman in the picture? Point out the diversity in your family—the varying shades of skin tone or the fact that only two other people have your son's red hair.

How to Talk to Your Grade School–Age Child

By grade school, children want to learn the connection between pictures and themselves. They're interested in relationships and want you to explain who everyone is. At this stage, a powerful visual tool is a family tree to diagram or illustrate your family lineage. Specific characteristics, both physical and psychological, can be traced. We encourage you to take time to design one of your own family. It is not only an excellent vehicle for self-exploration but also a way to involve your children in discovering various characteristics of their family history. A particular feature, like hair color, or a behavior, like assertiveness, can be traced. You can use a family tree to uncover the source of some of the images, values, and ideas that have been shaping your family for generations. You might find surprising strengths.

But remember that a family tree can be a very sensitive tool. You're using it to explore deeply personal characteristics of people who are important to you, some of whom will still be alive. You'll want to be considerate in your evaluation, in how you discuss your feelings with your children. Your goal is not to humiliate, expose, or degrade anyone who might not have contributed positively toward your development. You simply want to become aware of the impact people might have had on you and how this influences your relationship with your children. To that end, it's crucial you use sensitivity in the telling.

How to Talk to Your Adolescent

At this point, your diagram of a family tree will no longer be enough. Your adolescent child will want clear explanations for why Grandpa can be explosive and Grandma sometimes drinks too much. You don't have to wait until your children are adolescents to begin to share with them some of your family of origin issues. Some children are mature enough to hear it while still in grade school. You have to know your child.

Our client Zelda struggled with this issue with her two daughters.

Zelda had been sexually abused by her uncle when she was a teenager. He had also had a drinking problem, and when he recovered, his behavior toward her stopped. As an adult, Zelda had been able to forgive him, but she still worried for her daughters' safety. Since Zelda lived near her aunt and uncle, the girls often wanted to visit their great-aunt, whom they thought of as a grandmother. Zelda always accompanied them. But when they were preteens, developing into young women, Zelda thought it time to tell them what had happened to her, for their own protection. Although she had talked to them over the years about sexual abuse, she had not told them about her uncle. She sat the girls down and explained to them that their great-uncle had touched her in inappropriate ways when she was around their age, and she wanted them to be aware that no one, not even their relative, was allowed to do that.

Though Zelda had been anxious about revealing this to them, the girls handled it well. They didn't stop loving their great-uncle, but they had an appropriate level of awareness about an issue that, tragically, all too many young women have to face. Zelda's honesty when they were old enough to process the information will protect her daughters in ways that no family member had been able to do for Zelda at the same age.

Now, these are not rigid guidelines. Once again, you have to know your child's maturity level. If your six-year-old comes to you wanting to know why Grandma smells funny and can't take care of him, you'd be doing your child a disservice if you pretended your mother didn't have a drinking problem or, worse, denied your child's observations. You don't need to launch into a speech about how difficult it was growing up in the home of an alcoholic, how horribly Grandma treated you when she was drunk, and on and on. But you should say something like "Yes, Grandma does smell funny sometimes when she drinks alcohol. When she does, she can't take care of you because it makes her feel sick."

Living the First Principle

Sometimes you have to focus on negative memories in order to confront them honestly. If healing is necessary, don't be afraid to let it begin or seek professional help to guide you further. If most of your memories are positive, as many parents' are, open your eyes to your real blessings. Either way, share your past with your parenting partner and your children so that they can see the spirit within you and gain useful insights for their journey through life with you.

2

Make Peace with Your Partner: The Second Principle

I accept my parenting partner for the person he/she is. We do not always have to agree in order to be a cooperative team. I will show my appreciation for my partner and learn to reciprocate.

Getting in Sync

People tend to think that team spirit comes naturally, especially for couples. But bonding well as a husband and wife doesn't mean that you automatically think and act as a team.

You can be great friends and great lovers, but being great parents requires the ability to manage a difficult and very specific partnership. Even partners who are generally loving and supportive toward each other have to work at being true parenting partners.

What sorts of parents, then, can create good teams for the benefit of their children? Actually, most parents—whether married, single, separated, or divorced—can. If you and your partner are motivated to make your children a priority, you will learn a lot from this chapter about how to raise the level of team spirit in your home.

Tim and Paula, for instance, thought they had as much team spirit as they needed in their family until one recent incident caught them by surprise.

> *Tim had always wanted a minibike as a boy, so when his son, T.J., expressed an interest, Tim was thrilled at the chance to share his old dream with his son. They went shopping one day without telling Mom and found just the right bike.*
>
> *Tim was out with T.J. taking it for a test run when Paula drove by on her way home from work. She called out the car window, "You guys be careful! Who does that bike belong to, anyway?"*
>
> *Tim and T.J. drove a little less enthusiastically into the driveway, where they met a puzzled and worried Paula. When Tim confessed that the bike was T.J.'s, she was livid that her husband had made such a significant purchase without her input. T.J. was both confused and disappointed by his mother's reaction. He wondered what the fuss was about.*
>
> *But Tim told her she was overreacting. Hadn't they always talked about being able to give their children the things they couldn't have as children? Tim felt this was an opportunity to bond with his son. Paula felt they needed to teach T.J. that he had to earn such extravagant gifts. She also was hurt that she hadn't been consulted and worried that T.J. could get hurt.*

Tim and Paula were not troubled by internal stresses, such as:

* Difficulty in balancing home life and work
* The absence of a partner in child rearing

- An illness or other factor that affects a family member physically or emotionally
- The child's personality, special condition, or disability

Still, they realized that they needed to work on forgiveness, acceptance, and team-spirited co-parenting.

To determine how in sync you are, observe your interaction with your partner this week. If you are divorced or separated, note your interactions when you have contact by visits or phone. Try to pinpoint areas of conflict. Also note areas in which you're satisfied. At the end of the week, answer *Yes* or *No* to the following statements.

1. We discuss our strategies for dealing with problems that come up.
2. We talk to our children together as a team.
3. We discipline our children in a consistent manner.
4. We spend time together with our children.
5. We attend school functions.
6. We make plans for their future together.
7. We attend extracurricular and sports events.
8. We observe family traditions.
9. We acknowledge and celebrate our children's achievements.
10. We are respectful and considerate toward each other.

If you answered no to two or more of these statements, you are wise to realize that you need to begin to work toward developing greater team spirit in your relationship.

If possible, encourage your child's other parent to answer the questions above for him- or herself, either with you or separately. Being candid in your answers and especially being willing to share them with each other is itself an extremely positive sign that you are operating as a team already, not as individuals in the same or separate households.

How Is Your Parent-to-Parent Relationship Affecting Your Child?

Maybe you think that your partnership or lack thereof will have little or no impact on your child. What we know about child development tells us otherwise. Children will show how they feel through their behavior even when they aren't verbally expressing themselves. Your relationship and interactions affect how they feel and behave. In order to feel safe and secure, children need stability and positive experiences. How parents resolve conflict and express caring and concern affects how children relate to the world. For example, when you're annoyed or aggravated by your partner, do you withdraw or ignore him or her? Your child may be picking up this style of responding to conflict. If you yell and scream during disagreements, it's likely your child does, too.

Is your relationship with your child's other parent affecting your child? Answer *Yes* or *No* to the following statements in order to find out.

1. When the two of you disagree in front of your child, you observe changes in your child's emotions or behavior.

2. Your child becomes anxious when the two of you discuss differences of opinion.

3. The two of you demonstrate love, caring, and affection in front of your child.

4. Your child expresses feelings of sadness about your family life.

5. Your child is clingy and appears insecure when separating from either of you.

6. Your child seeks a great deal of attention when the two of you are engaged in conversation.

7. Your child describes or draws pictures of family members as happy.

8. Your child is receptive to your organizing and making plans for family activities.

9. Your child shows unprovoked anger and frustration toward siblings.

10. At times you observe your child emulating a negative style of relating that the two of you have modeled.

If you answered yes to 1, 2, 4, 5, 6, 9, or 10 or no to 3, 7, or 8, your relationship is problematic. Most couples occasionally expose their children to problems and challenges that the children don't need to know about. This is normal. But frequent, pervasive, and continuous exposure leads to excessive anxiety, confusion, distrust, and fear.

Children do need to see and understand that all families have challenges or problems to face and deal with. They should witness that it's okay to disagree and still love and care for each other. Parents can show children how to manage feelings of anger and frustration effectively, without losing control or becoming hostile.

If you did the work of Chapter 1, you recognize that issues from your past are playing themselves out and affecting your views and attitudes toward parenting your child. The question to ask yourself now is how family of origin issues could be affecting your sense of team spirit with your partner.

Do You Believe That Mother Knows Best?

Gender stereotypes continue to be a common holdover from our families of origin.

For example, most women tend to think they can parent better or more quickly than men. Like not trusting a man's ability to do the laundry properly (the way a woman would do it), a mother may question a dad's nurturing or disciplinary skills.

The stereotypical view that women parent best has been fostered in our society for years. Fathers were the breadwinners and mothers handled the daily parenting responsibilities. Even though some men are now looking to other men for validation, support, and guidance in assuming more initiative in the home, most men assume that a mother has primary responsibility for child rearing.

> When Brad's daughter Carol was having trouble learning to read in first grade, he blamed his wife, Blanche, because she's a stay-at-home mom. He felt it was her responsibility to teach the children, since she was home with them. But Blanche believed that Brad was more educated and therefore the better teacher. She also resented Brad's implication that because she didn't work outside the home, she had tons of free time and was making poor use of it.

It would be wrong, of course, to say that one's gender has no unique impact or vantage point in parenting. Men and women frequently have categorically different experiences and skills, despite sharing insight, empathy, and understanding. These differences should prove very helpful in guiding your children as they come to recognize gender differences. For example, as a parent team, we sometimes draw upon a male or female perspective when attempting to understand a problem our son or daughter is having.

But it's important to avoid the attitude that simply by being one gender or the other, you're a better parent or you should know more about parenting emotionally, intellectually, or instinctively. Only a woman can be a great mother and a man can be a great father, but members of both genders can be great parents.

Before problems in your relationship grow, discuss your mutual expectations about a mother's role. Pay attention to your different backgrounds, experiences, or upbringings. Define what works best for you as partners, given your marital status, individual talents, skills, and preferences. Keep in mind fairness and balance. If you're tied too rigidly to what your mother did earlier or what seems to be the way most people are functioning around you, you are missing this opportunity to grow as a team. Be willing to experiment with different arrangements for the betterment of your family.

Do You Think That Father Knows Best?

It stands to reason that you and your partner are not going to think alike on many aspects of traditional fatherhood, either. You came from different households, possibly from different parts of the country or the world. You had different parenting and personal experiences while growing up. You might have had different levels of education or occupations, and inevitably you're going to have different views. This is probably even more pronounced if you're divorced or co-parenting.

For instance, if a mother thinks it is the father's role to play the heavy and discipline, as in "Wait until your father gets home," she will resent it if he's permissive. So what happens if she disagrees with him on the appropriate amount of discipline? Consider Mark and Betty's story.

Mark had it up to here with what he considered "soft" parenting. His brand was tough love, which included spankings on a regular basis. He frequently remarked to Betty, "I had my share of beatings when I was growing up, and I didn't become a wife beater or ax murderer." What he failed to see was how his children were beginning to be more aggressive toward each other and were getting into fights at school. This led to spankings at home for problems at school and punishments for not getting along with their siblings. The negative cycle of spankings, sibling conflicts at home, and aggressive behavior at school seemed impossible to break. Betty wanted peace and harmony with Mark and so chose to accept Mark's view of child rearing.

When the school called to inform them of yet another playground fight involving their children, Betty asked Mark if they could seek counseling. He agreed, because he was becoming confused as to why the kids couldn't control themselves better. It became clear in counseling that Mark's philosophy was not effective. Betty had not shared her view with Mark until she sat in our office. She believed that a firm but more positive approach might work and that spanking was not the answer. We gave both of them the task of identifying a structure or goal for the children, such as doing something nice for each other and not hitting when they were angry. Next, we asked them to discuss discipline techniques that included a mixture of positive reward and negative consequence. This combined Mark's belief that punishment might be necessary and Betty's philosophy that you can get more from children with a positive approach.

Accept that through genetics and experiences you and your partner will have different views, yet you can still find common ground.

Are You Divided by Spiritual Faith?

The most frequent issue that divides couples is religion. Where there's diversity in faith, peace will require respect and resistance to the feeling that one person's religion is more important or better than the other's. The major pathways to spirituality are equally wide.

The right ways to deal with differences in religious backgrounds are limited only by your willingness to be open and creative. For example, one couple we worked with have combined his Jewish faith and her Catholic faith to allow their children to participate in the rituals of both. They celebrate Hanukkah and Christmas. For another couple, the wife converted to her spouse's religion, and for still another, the wife is raising their child in her faith while the husband maintains his own faith but doesn't worship regularly. Though the methods may vary, the keys are understanding, acceptance, and agreement with one another. By your example, your children will experience the meaning of spiritual faith and learn the life lesson of acceptance of differences.

Is Your Parenting Style Competitive?

Competitive parenting is divisive. It places your child in the center of a tug-of-war. Each parent thinks he or she wins in a contest of wills and words. Typically, the outcome of such a situation is either that one partner finally gives in or the issue remains unresolved indefinitely, creating stress and uncertainty for your child.

By contrast, cooperative parenting requires negotiation and compromise. Cooperative parenting requires you to:

1. Listen to your partner's views in private without interrupting or judging.

2. Express your view without dismissing your partner's.

3. Present a compromise.

4. Negotiate by giving up some part of what you want for something your partner wants.

5. Agree on the compromise and follow through like a team.

If, as your children grow, they become more aware that their parents are more competitive than cooperative, they will begin to use this to their advantage. Children naturally try to manipulate parents to get their own way. This divide-and-conquer approach is quite natural. But it's your job as a parent to make sure that it fails. That will not be easy if you and your partner wage a subtle battle against each other.

John and Julie came to us confused and concerned because they felt they had lost control over their children's behavior. When asked to do any small task, their children would often answer, "I don't want to" or "I don't have to." John and Julie were worried that their children were headed for trouble. They were right, but upon examination, they learned the problem did not rest as much with their children as with the situation they had created as parents. John and Julie were caught up in competitive parenting. Both wanted their children to see them as the more giving, understanding, and loving parent. It was commonplace for both parents to discover that, contrary to each one's preference, somehow an item that was supposed to be earned by their child would be given without discussion or consideration by the other parent. Still, Julie declared on a regular basis that her children would learn the value of working hard or at least behaving properly to earn privileges and rewards. However, the children had learned they could short-circuit this by appealing to Dad. John had come to be viewed by the children as the "good" parent, who always let them have their way.

Parents who compete will try to gain the approval, love, and loyalty of a child by giving in or siding with the child over the other parent. But the children are hurt. They identify one parent as the "good" parent and the other as the "bad" parent. What results are children who are likely to be disrespectful toward both parents and rely on manipulation to get what they want.

Team-spirited parents—it's worth repeating—strive, by contrast, to cooperate in support of each other's decisions. They make their best efforts to present a united front and always discuss differences privately. They negotiate and compromise. After this process, they agree on an approach with their children. Fortunately for John and Julie, by learning to outline their goals for their children together—both long-term and short-term goals—they were eventually able to put their competitive parenting tendencies behind them. Their children quickly adjusted and improved their behavior.

When you compete with your partner, it is usually a symptom of how your past has affected your parenting style. Remember whom you identified with most in your family and what that person's parenting style was like. Think about the attitudes that person held about children. List the negative and positive messages. Challenge the negatives and embrace the positives.

Are You "Parallel Parenting"?

You have probably heard the term "parallel play," usually to refer to the developmental period of toddlerhood, when one child plays next to her peer but rarely with her peer. Both may build with blocks, but it doesn't yet occur to them that they can build a better tower together. Parallel parenting works similarly. It means you do your own thing without consulting or considering your partner.

Can two parents raise the same children in totally different ways? Not if they want stable children.

Sometimes parents are afraid to assert their ideals about parenting to their partner, so one partner will choose to do it her own way when the other partner isn't around—or even if he is. Little effort is made on either part to join or combine efforts in child rearing. Maybe a parent feels too threatened or perceives this as too difficult to do. Maybe he or she doesn't see how valuable or important it is to work as a cooperative and united team.

In a sense, parallel parenting is connected to competitive parenting, in that there is no interest or willingness—and in some cases, a lack of awareness—of how and why to include others (primarily the partner) in the child-rearing process. Parallel parenting occurs most often when the idea of working in partnership with someone else seems threatening. One or both parents have a sense of inadequacy and a lack of skill at being a team player.

The net result is that each parent will feel quite alone, isolated, and unsupported.

In a quiet moment before you're facing your next parenting crisis, answer these questions. Did your parents seem to work together as a team, or did one of them seem to control most of the child rearing? Who did the following tasks?

- Nurturing
- Disciplining
- Organizing family social events
- Deciding how leisure time was spent

Is the pattern that you see cooperative, competitive, or parallel? If you were exposed to a mostly competitive style, you may find yourself struggling to appreciate and respect the differences in your partner's parenting style. You may intentionally or unintentionally undermine it and otherwise try to prove that your approach is superior. This competitiveness may lead to further complications if your partner chooses not to compete by becoming passive or by engaging in a parallel style.

Unless you work together, you and your partner may spend more time consulting experts and family members and buying collections of books that support your approach to parenting than in forming a more effective and efficient parenting team. Team spirit, on the other hand, assumes openness to learning and working in a cooperative manner. It doesn't allow either you or your partner to work against each other.

Are You Ever the Martyr?

When you examined your own background, did you remember a parent who routinely sacrificed and who may on occasion have sacrificed to an extreme? Do expressions like "After all I did for you" and "You'll finally appreciate me when I'm gone" sound familiar?

The 180-degree opposite of a competitive parent is a parent who makes sacrifice an art form. That parent gets perverse pleasure in fostering guilt feelings in her partner and children. This kind of motivation is not at all constructive.

A parent who is a martyr is one who cannot set limits. She feels she has to do the entire act of child rearing, as a superparent. She doesn't allow herself to relinquish or even delegate certain responsibilities. Her partner plays second string and minimizes his involvement.

> *Sharon loved teaching but gave up her career to support her husband, Malcolm, in building his dental practice. She would care for their children while doing his billing and paperwork late at night. Whenever something needed to be done with the children at school or some extracurricular event, Sharon volunteered. Sharon was admired by all her friends for her amazing ability to juggle so much and support her husband so well. But Sharon was slowly becoming dissatisfied with her life, and it was starting to show in her short-tempered treatment of Malcolm and their children. What she really wanted most, but had become unable to voice in her martyrdom, was to return to teaching.*
>
> *Sharon finally acknowledged that she no longer wanted to do the paperwork for Malcolm. When she voiced her concerns and needs to him and stopped engaging in enabling behavior, the couple was able to discuss her needs as well as his. Sharon returned to work, Malcolm hired an office manager, and the children enjoyed a happier mother.*

The martyr takes on more responsibility than she thinks is fair, yet she experiences a kind of joy in playing the role of put-upon parent. Clearly this is a big obstacle to family harmony. The mother or father who takes on most of the responsibility gets a small payback in feelings of importance, even though he or she resents it. Others view this person as self-sacrificing and committed, and the person gets positive attention from this dynamic. However, he or she frequently feels overwhelmed and harbors resentment and anger at what's viewed to be a lack of support, interest, and desire to be involved as a parent.

Overcoming the problem of martyrdom starts with an awareness of the pattern. If you're the martyr, typically you will be codependent. That means you enable others around you to support you in your role by being a complaining but persistent people pleaser. Sometimes your true reaction will manifest itself in more complaints, such as getting sick so that you have to say no to hosting the PTA dinner.

A perceptive partner will observe your behavior and offer support, but martyrs don't relinquish the role easily. You may be ambivalent because of the benefits and privileges of being in charge of everything. Once you and your partner are aware of this pattern, you have to stop enabling. For instance, if your children are supposed to clean their rooms, you can't consistently do it for them.

Do You Sabotage Your Partner?

Sabotage occurs when you allow feelings of anger, resentment, jealousy, or rejection to interfere with your child's best interests, for example, when one parent shows distance and resentment toward the other by interfering with his or her decisions. Sabotage is more likely to take place when no true agreement or mutual investment and commitment to a decision has been reached by parenting partners. One might be overly critical of the other or resist by not following through in support of the decision.

This is usually done in a passive-aggressive or indirect way—like forgetting to honor commitments or giving a gift to one child and not another. These are attempts to "get back" at the other parent or the child.

We saw this with Sherry, who is a competitive swimmer with dreams of making the Olympic team.

> *Sherry's parents have been heavily involved in her training and development. When they began to have marital problems, her father minimized his involvement. Her mother had been a competitive swimmer and strongly encouraged Sherry to continue. Because of the father's anger toward his wife, he began to sabotage Sherry's ambition.*

Displacing anger toward a parenting partner onto a child leads to dysfunctional relationship patterns. You have to be aware of a tendency to interfere and sabotage. If this pattern sounds familiar, you need to develop alternate ways of handling your anger that do not compromise your child or your partner's ability to be a good parent.

Are You the Insecure Teammate?

As we have seen, parenting can be made more difficult if one parent doesn't trust his or her ability. This insecure parent avoids taking responsibility by leaving most parenting tasks to the other parent. He might manifest this by ignoring an issue while looking to the other parent to handle it. For example, a notice from school comes home, and instead of discussing it with the child and contacting the teacher, the insecure parent leaves it on the kitchen table for the other parent to address. He does not feel competent to take steps to deal with it. There may even be thoughts such as "What if I do the wrong thing? I'm not sure what the right thing is." This insecurity paralyzes an insecure parent against taking action to solve a problem. And it builds resentment in the other parent, who feels that all parenting responsibilities rest on her slightly more confident shoulders.

None of us have complete confidence in our ability to parent successfully. You don't have to pass a test or fulfill licensing requirements to become a parent. When the time comes, all of us are insecure about the kind of parents we'll be. To succeed, we must first acknowledge and tap in to each other's strengths. Then, jointly, we can tackle each parenting challenge. For example, one partner may have a knack for figuring out specific steps to solve a problem. The other partner's strength may be in making the process happen in a compassionate and cooperative way that helps the family as a whole commit to the solution.

However, it's important not only that partners understand and accept their own limitations but that they understand, accept, and empathize with *each other's* limitations. Providing mutual support is a very necessary and positive practice, even more so if one partner is trying to deal with feelings of insecurity or, worse, a chronic litany of self-criticism.

Are You Divorced or Separated?

Trying to work around someone else's perception of parenting—indeed, of you—when it's antithetical to all you hoped you'd accomplish as a parent can be one of the most painful experiences you may undergo as you struggle to raise your children.

Divorced and separated couples often have great difficulty making peace with one another. Typically, there are some residual feelings of resentment and bitterness regarding the issues leading to separation and/or divorce. Making peace involves accepting some of those differences and moving beyond them for the betterment of the children.

Even in the friendliest separations, the caregiving parent faces special issues. Take Gina, for instance.

Gina realizes how much her son loves the contact he has with his father. Although she had her differences with her ex-husband, she makes every effort to involve him in their son's life. Whenever she schedules doctor visits, school meetings, vacations, and birth-day parties, she makes sure to inform Jess, her ex, and ask for his input and involvement.

Recently a wonderful career opportunity arose that required her to relocate from Boston to Jacksonville, Florida. Gina very much wants to accept it, but how can her son have ongoing con-tact with Jess? It has to be a lot more difficult to share decision-making and child-rearing responsibilities via telephone, e-mail, letters, and infrequent visits. But what about her needs? Can she work as a team with her ex with such a geographical distance between them?

Of course she can, but clearly it's going to require more work and more consideration than before. A big advantage for Gina and Jess is that they have enough mutuality in their relationship to build a team approach to raising their son.

It's a serious question: How do you focus on what's best for your child when you can't get along with your partner at all?

The rest of your child's life might depend on how you answer this. It may be tough to face the fact that the issues that led to the end of your rela-tionship will crop up in a future discussion or negotiation with your child's other parent. But you must try. Staying focused on what's in the best inter-ests of your child is the primary aim of your self-sacrifice. Another is to develop a co-parenting arrangement that maintains and enhances your child's quality of life.

If the reality of your relationship doesn't allow for discussion, send this book to your child's other parent. Highlight the affirmation at the opening of this chapter. In a letter to your partner, write down your hopes for the future regarding co-parenting. Let it be a new beginning. Start with forgiveness and acceptance that the past be the past. Ask and express this concern: What do you want for your children now?

Making peace with your partner starts with an attitude of partnership. Whether you really like the situation or not, if that other person is involved with your child, you're partners in parenting.

Of course, we realize that you may harbor insurmountable feelings of resentment and anger toward your ex. If so, you should be clear with your children that reconciliation is not possible. But also be equally clear that demonstrating team-spirited care, civility, and concern is essential. Practice saying this to your children and parenting partner. When you show disdain, apathy, disinterest, or distance from your parenting partner, you may rationalize by saying, "At least I'm not hostile or overtly disrespectful." Even so, your behavior is still confusing if not damaging to your child. Try stopping the confusion and damage now.

Write yourself a letter stating all the reasons you find it difficult to make peace. For example, "I'm angry with him." "I still resent her." "She's so deceitful." "He's selfish." "He was abusive toward me." "She was unfaithful." "He doesn't pay child support regularly."

Look at pictures of your children. Look at your children. Which do you value more, your feelings or your child?

Rip up the letter or burn it. "Funeralize" it by burying it.

When these feelings or issues surface again, do the writing process once more. Write another letter with positive affirmations of what it will be like for your children when you make peace with your partner in parenting. Most likely, they will experience increased feelings of security, safety, love, nurturance, and peace—just what all parents want for their children.

Are You the Parent Who Works a Lot?

Modern life stresses even long-standing marriages, when business trips routinely take a mother or father away for days and sometimes weeks or more. That places a substantial roadblock to parenting as a team. Not only is this hard for the parent who's away, it can be difficult for the parent at home when the traveling parent returns to unintentionally mess up the new routine.

Trying to balance the demands of a job that requires travel with the joys and responsibilities of being with children is one of the most difficult dilemmas couples are facing today. And we're not talking just about a father's absence, because as more women become part of the workforce— especially in professional and executive positions—mothers, too, are being pulled in opposing directions. Parents in this situation are constantly weighing the advantages of a job that may be interesting and offer financial rewards versus absences from children and the inability to be part of their daily lives.

Being a team parent doesn't necessarily mean quitting your job, but it does mean being patient with one another. It's crucial for the family separated by time and space to reconnect continually, via telephone or e-mail while you're away from home and with rituals when you return. The parent who is at home may need a short period of time when the other returns to shed his or her single-parent mode. Work together to come up with ways to do so. The returning parent may need rituals to reconnect with children and a partner he or she has been absent from.

With the frequently absent parent, discuss developing a smooth reentry routine. For instance, always set aside time just to listen and encourage a mutual sharing of feelings and events. Spend as much time as it takes (usually less than you might think) for bonding to occur between you and family members.

How Compassionate Are You?

When you're willing to work together as a team, even when one of you is having a day filled with fouls, the other will be able to help keep you both in the game.

Team-spirited parents learn through years of practice to capitalize on each other's strengths and minimize each other's weaknesses. For example, if Dad tends to get too emotional or angry when talking to the soccer coach who doesn't allow Johnny to play, Mom and Dad can figure out what helps Dad to stay cool. If Dad starts to go overboard, he can step back and let Mom be the assertive one. If Mom is exhausted after a long day of business meetings and just has no patience left for making dinner and helping the kids with homework, Dad can cook or order a pizza and help with Cindy's math problems while Mom puts her feet up for a few refreshing moments.

To be this creative requires that you also be compassionate toward one another. We all make mistakes, have bad days, show poor judgment, over-react, or just plain mess up at times. When you are compassionate, you don't berate or belittle the person who has faulted, but offer the support they need to get beyond the moment.

It's important for your children to see you show compassion for one another. This can be particularly difficult in the heat of a conflict. However, you can always go back and apologize, showing forgiveness and tenderness. It's a valuable lesson for your children to hear you apologize in front of them for an argument they overheard.

Do You Know How to Give and Take Criticism?

To be creative, compassionate partners, you also need to be able to discuss your differences constructively. Because this process may involve criticism, it can make you both feel uncomfortable. So it's extremely important to communicate in a sensitive and caring manner.

Avoid blaming or dumping piles of complaints. Always begin by pointing out positives.

Remind yourself that however much in love you were, however strong your relationship still is, and however committed you are to being good parents, you are still individuals. No parents share identical ideas and views about parenting. You must accept this as a natural course of human development. However close you are emotionally, socially, sexually, and politically, you couldn't possibly have had the same exact parenting experiences and family of origin issues. The experiences and issues were different, and so was the way they were handled. When it comes to your own parenting views, you may be a few inches or a few miles apart.

We want to stress that you and your partner must recognize your differences as parents. Developing empathy, compassion, and understanding of the differences is crucial. Once you recognize and accept what divides you as parents, you can work to close the gaps, and in the meantime you can strengthen the views and feelings and actions that unite you.

Fred, a person with whom we're working, provides an example.

Fred frequently observed angry confrontations between his parents. His father was distracted and forgetful—for example, not remembering to pick up Fred or his brother from basketball prac-

tice—and not the best at following through on commitments. This infuriated Fred's mother, and she wouldn't hesitate to yell at her husband about it.

Usually his father would take the criticism with nothing more than a "shut up" tossed in, but there were a few times he got so angry himself that he would put his hand over his wife's face and press her head against the wall. Frank and his younger brother would become very frightened and were poised to run to a neighbor's house or call the police.

Now Fred is a father himself. Whenever he is criticized by his own wife, especially in front of the children, his immediate reaction is to say "shut up" and then storm out of the house. He thinks he's being belittled and humiliated in their children's eyes. Fred also leaves because he doesn't want to become physical the way his father did.

What we've been working on with Fred is first to have him acknowledge the issues from his childhood that are influencing his feelings today—and not only his feelings but also his actions. It seems that at times Fred is willfully irresponsible, as if to invite his wife's criticism, repeating a pattern.

Second, we are working with Fred and his wife so that he can better express his feelings, so that she understands how her criticism is especially destructive, and to help her to gain empathy and understanding of her husband. In other respects they have a very strong relationship and consider each other good parents, so our task is to build on the strengths and resolve the parenting issue that divides their team.

Determine how you can use your individual strengths more strategically to form a stronger team. List your expectations, strengths, and weaknesses. List your partner's. Here are two questions to help you generate discussion and insight:

1. In what areas of parenting do you depend on your parenting partner or look to your partner for leadership?

2. What are the areas of parenting for which you think your partner looks to you?

When to Seek Professional Help

Some of the parenting attitudes and styles we examined in this chapter will be easier to reverse than others. Working together, you should be able to discuss the gender perspectives and worldviews you both hold and reach an understanding, if not an agreement, about the things that separate you. This will be more difficult, though not impossible, if the issues that separate you have more to do with your styles. If you're a competitive parent, if you practice parallel parenting, if you sabotage your relationship, or if you are a martyr or an insecure parent, your task will be more challenging. Chances are it's not just your parenting you need to concern yourself with, but your views and feelings about your partner as well.

Children may emulate a parent's insecurity or self-defeating style. This leads to feelings of low self-esteem and a lack of productiveness. Overcoming your insecurities before they affect your children not only involves self-awareness of your style but entails gaining parenting knowledge and developing skills. Reading books, attending parenting workshops and forums, and talking to other supportive parents will give you a sense of empowerment and confidence. If you have a continued sense of hopelessness and inadequacy, we recommend you try individual counseling. It may also be beneficial to seek marriage counseling.

Obviously, not all disagreements in parenting style require outside help. For example, you may never totally embrace the fact that your partner likes to have your children keep everything in order while you're more comfortable with a reasonable amount of disarray. And you can live with that.

But some disagreements do require professional attention.

For instance, one partner may have come from a background where the parents believed "Spare the rod, spoil the child." As a result, this partner may be abusive toward the children. Of course, accepting this background doesn't mean that the other partner must accept the behavior.

Don't let your children be victims. Step up to the plate with the leadership to seek help.

Living the Second Principle

When you're able to make peace with your partner, you allow your family the grace of blooming into a healthy, loving unit. As you travel the path of parenting with the same goals in mind, you can better express your needs to each other and to your children. And if your first priority is the emotional health of your family, the possibilities for your children's futures are limitless.

3

Communicate Compassionately: The Third Principle

I will communicate my feelings openly, clearly, directly, and also respectfully of my parenting partner, because this encourages honest, meaningful, and positive dialogue within my family.

Couple Communication Skills

Every couple—whether married or divorced—speaks a unique language that develops over time. You have your jokes that no one else would understand, even if you tried to share them. You may have private nicknames for one another. You have a rhythm that determines when each of you speaks and for how long. You know who is more comfortable with long discussions and who likes to get straight to the point. Even if you are not living with your parenting partner, you still have an established style of communicating with each other.

But couples also have their communication gaps, those moments when one or both of you want to shout, "Isn't anyone listening to me?" At those moments all the communication rules you've established can fly out the window. Those are the moments when:

- Even if your partner is listening to you, he's completely misunderstood what you're saying.
- You feel as if one of you is speaking another language.
- Neither of you seems to have time to really listen to the other.
- You realize that you're kinder and more polite to strangers than you are to your parenting partner.
- You realize your conversation is escalating into a quarrel.

Moments like these are perfectly normal. Sometimes bad communication is just a natural, temporary by-product of different personalities living together. But your team is in trouble if misunderstandings are the steady state. Parenting partners start to drift apart when they stop being able to talk to each other. As you and your partner communicate less and less about the issues that affect your relationship, you grow more likely to stop talking as much as you need to about your children. You may unwittingly fall into communication patterns that are harmful to your family unit.

If you and your child's other parent are already living apart, communication may be a strained affair right now. If so, beware of assuming that words don't matter. Work that communication muscle.

When you have children, the pace of family life can be challenging. However, partners in parenting have to make time to discuss issues and make decisions together. How are you and your partner communicating with each other? Take a moment to find out.

1. Do you find that you have little time to discuss issues about your children?

2. Do you make decisions without remembering to include your partner?

3. Do you initiate dialogue about your children?

4. Do you listen attentively when your partner is talking and try to reflect or paraphrase what was said?

5. Do you validate your partner's feelings by verbalizing understanding of how he or she feels even if you disagree with the issue being discussed?

6. Do you interrupt you partner when he or she is talking?

7. Do you bring up old grievances or problems when discussing a current issue?

8. Do you engage in destructive communication, such as nasty comments or name-calling?

If you answered yes to questions 1, 2, 6, 7, or 8 or no to questions 3, 4, or 5, there are areas of your communication that can be improved.

Remember that conflict and communication gaps are a natural part of all relationships. Neither should be interpreted as a sign that your communication styles are incompatible. The steps for compassionate communicating that we've outlined in this chapter can help anyone become a better communicator.

Understand Your Different Communication Styles

If you're wondering why you and your partner are disagreeing, or if you're frustrated because you can't make yourself understood, the first step to improving matters is to take a look at exactly what your individual communication styles are.

Most people tend to communicate in one of four styles. These are passive, aggressive, passive-aggressive, and assertive. None of us relates consistently in any one style. It's likely that you vacillate between styles. However, there's usually one style you'll lean toward most often. Consider this hypothetical situation: Your daughter has been begging you to let her get her ears pierced. You and your partner had agreed that when she brought her grades up, then you'd discuss it. Her grades have been wonderful this semester, so you want to reward her. The only problem is that your partner hasn't been home much lately. He's been working on an important project at work. You don't want to bother him about this decision, particularly since you both already agreed on the outcome. You waffle for a few minutes, then glance at your daughter's expectant face and grab the car keys, telling her, "Come on. It's time you got your ears pierced." But when your partner sees your daughter, he explodes. "How could you go ahead with this without discussing it with me?" How do you respond?

1. You apologize and promise never to make a decision without him again. This is a passive response.

2. You get angry and say, "Well, you're never around anymore, so I'm making the decisions on my own." This is an aggressive approach.

3. You seethe inwardly and say nothing, but plan ways to punish him for losing his temper with you. This is passive-aggressive behavior.

4. You tell him directly and clearly how you feel. "I feel bad that I went ahead with this decision when you were unable to be here to discuss it. But we had agreed this was what we would do. Let's talk about our schedules and decision making." This response is assertive and is an effective way to express feelings and thoughts without attacking or withdrawing from others. You invite discussion and create the possibility of resolving conflicts.

Let's look at some detailed examples of how individuals who have these styles tend to behave.

1. **Passive people don't express feelings openly and, as a result, usually neglect their own needs.** They behave in a way that tells the family, "Don't pay attention to me. Your needs always come first." They will apologize for their actions, do almost anything to avoid confrontation, and make excuses because they don't know how to be direct. Nonverbal clues, such as speaking in a weak voice, failure to make eye contact, clammy hands, and excess fidgeting often betray their inhibitions.

   > *Lanie is always in a crisis, always needing something from her husband, never able to make a decision without consulting him. She's overly dependent, but she is not passive. She always expresses her needs. Al resents her dependency but is passive in how he deals with it. He always takes over when Lanie becomes hysterical about something. He leaves important business meetings early to help her cope with situations she should be able to handle on her own. Al has a very stressful job and would like nothing more than to come home and feel confident that another crisis won't be awaiting him. Yet he doesn't complain, because he sees himself as the good guy. He just can't say no.*
   >
   > *But he reacts nonetheless. He and Lanie are no longer intimate, and he has begun spending more time with a female co-worker who places no demands on him.*
   >
   > *Al may not realize it, but his passivity is putting his marriage on the line. How much better it would be if he spoke with Lanie about his resentment of her dependence. It would be no guarantee that their marriage would survive, but it*

would be a positive move toward compassionate communi-cation for both of them.

2. **Aggressive people are often openly hostile or rude in defense of their own interests.** Their feelings come first, and they go to extremes to make certain they get their own way. Tactics used to dominate a partner often include sarcastic responses, put-downs, and shrill verbal attacks. The nonverbal signals of an aggressive response include finger-pointing, talking with the hands, putting hands on hips, moving the head from side to side, and scowling.

   A typical example of the aggressive style would be the abusive spouse. But anyone who just wants to get an issue off his or her chest and expects the partner to pick up the pieces has an aggressive communication style. Saying things like "You can't do anything right," engaging in name-calling, and making other kinds of hostile statements are all forms of verbal abuse. The new mother who constantly criticizes her husband for his clumsiness with the baby when in reality he just has no experience with diapering, for instance, is a person who is comfortable degrading her partner.

3. **Passive-aggressive people are manipulative and sometimes irresponsible because they won't state their emotions honestly but are nonetheless determined to get their own way.** Rather than saying no or explaining why they don't want to do something, they're indirect. For example, a woman may agree to a request and then do everything possible to sabotage it. A typical passive-aggressive response is for her to arrive late to an event she didn't want to attend or to forget about a commitment she made. Body language that often gives passive-aggressive people away includes rolling their eyes, folding their arms across their chest, and sighing a lot. Commonly, passive-aggressives displace their anger, lashing out at someone else or overreacting to an unrelated event.

4. **Assertive people express feelings and needs clearly and directly without lashing out or overlooking their partner's viewpoint.**

Assertive communication doesn't just concern itself with winning. The objective is not to overpower or dominate but to lay the groundwork for negotiation. Assertive communication involves the use of "I feel" statements. The assertive person makes direct eye contact and has a posture of openness.

For example, you have to work late, so you ask your husband to go to the dry cleaners and pick up a suit that you want to wear to a meeting tomorrow morning. When you get home, you discover he forgot to pick it up, and the dry cleaners is closed. Given that you realize there's little you can do except wear a different outfit tomorrow, and given that it's human nature to forget things from time to time, here's what the assertive communicator will say: "I'm really frustrated that I thought you were taking care of this for me and you forgot." And then let it go. Nothing would be gained except hard feelings if you were to adopt any of the other communication styles. If this is a chronic pattern with your partner, that, too, can be discussed in an assertive way: "It upsets me to feel I can't rely on you when I ask for help. Is there something we can do so this doesn't keep happening? Maybe it would help if I wrote notes to you and left them on your dresser? What do you think?"

With assertive communication, your partner's feelings or character are never attacked and you open the door to honesty and problem solving.

In order to recognize your own communication style, imagine the following situations and choose the response that most clearly matches the one you are likely to make:

1. Your partner arrives hours late for a family dinner celebrating your son's birthday that was scheduled days in advance. You say:

a) "It's okay. I'll just reheat the food."

b) "I'm upset that you were so late."

c) "Where the hell were you?"

d) "No big deal. But dinner's ruined."

2. Your partner shouts at the children whenever he wants them to finish their chores. You say:

a) "I guess somebody has to get the kids to do their chores, but my mother thinks you yell a lot."

b) "It seems as if you always yell at people."

c) "I like it better when you're firm with the children without yelling."

d) "I don't know why the children just won't listen to us."

3. Your teenage son has violated an agreed-upon curfew. You:

a) Ask him if he's eaten and ignore the fact that he avoided curfew.

b) Throw up your hands in frustration, walk away, and refuse to speak to him.

c) Enforce a punishment after you explain why you feel angry and disappointed.

d) Call him irresponsible and tell him he's grounded for a month.

4. Your partner wants to allow your seven-year-old son to watch an R-rated video. You say:

a) "Don't you dare let him watch that! What's wrong with you?"

b) "I read an article that said it's not a good idea to let children watch R-rated movies."

c) "Okay."

d) "I know you want to watch the video and also spend time with Bobby, but I don't feel comfortable with him watching it. Please watch it another time."

5. Your partner wants to spend more than you both agreed on for souvenirs while on vacation, but your budget is very tight. You say:

a) "Sure."

b) "No way. You're always wasting money."

c) "I understand that you want to do this, but we're on a tight budget, and I don't think we can spare the cash right now."

d) "I would like to, but my purse was stolen yesterday."

6. You're upset and angry because of a conflict at work, and you want emotional support from your partner and children. You say:

a) "I need a hug. This has been a very frustrating day, and I'd like to talk about it."

b) "Why can't you all be more sensitive?"

c) "Let's go out to dinner."

d) "Nothing's wrong."

7. Your partner's family believes in corporal punishment and thinks you indulge your children too much. You say:

a) "Your family is nuts."

b) "I love visiting your family" (even though you don't).

c) "I feel uneasy visiting your family when they yell at the kids and criticize our parenting."

d) "I don't feel well. I can't visit your family today."

8. You want to go to family therapy to improve communication and discipline techniques, but your partner refuses. You say:

a) "You're not committed to our kids."

b) "I feel disappointed when you won't go to therapy, because I really need your support and want you to be involved."

c) "You don't have to go."

d) "The therapist said if you don't come, the family will fall apart."

Here are the communication styles demonstrated by each response:

1. a) passive; b) assertive; c) aggressive; d) passive-aggressive

2. a) passive-aggressive; b) aggressive; c) assertive; d) passive

3. a) passive; b) passive-aggressive; c) assertive; d) aggressive

4. a) aggressive; b) passive-aggressive; c) passive; d) assertive

5. a) passive; b) aggressive; c) assertive; d) passive-aggressive

6. a) assertive; b) aggressive; c) passive-aggressive; d) passive

7. a) aggressive; b) passive; c) assertive; d) passive-aggressive

8. a) aggressive; b) assertive; c) passive; d) passive-aggressive

Add up the number of responses that fall under each category. Which style do you use most often? If five or more of your responses are not assertive, your communication skills may be creating a barrier to communicating compassionately with your child's other parent. Commit yourself to learning new assertive ways of talking to your partner—and your children.

On page 59 are some examples of dialogue ranging from aggressive to passive-aggressive to passive to assertive.

As long as your pattern of communication is most often assertive, you can be forgiven for those lapses in judgment when you wish later you could take back what you said.

How Do You Respond?

Aggressive	Passive-Aggressive	Passive	Assertive
"You made me angry."	"Sometimes you're mean to me."	"It doesn't bother me."	"I feel angry because you yelled at me."
"That comment was stupid."	"That comment doesn't make sense."	"Whatever you say is fine."	"I feel uncomfortable with what you said."
"Get out of my face."	"Why don't you go visit your friends?"	"I'm okay."	"I'm upset and need time to cool off."
"You'd better be home by six."	"I'm going to start eating at six."	"Whatever time you get home is fine."	"I'd really like it if you could be home by six."
"If you don't call to check on the kids by ten P.M., don't call."	"I send the kids to bed at ten P.M."	"Call us anytime."	"We're looking forward to your call. Please call before ten P.M."
"No, I don't want to go."	"I have a headache."	"Sure."	"No, thank you. I don't want to go today. But thanks for asking."
"You're such a jerk. I saw you roll your eyes."	"Let's go home."	"I guess they aren't making too much noise."	"I feel uncomfortable and disrespected when you roll your eyes while I'm disciplining the kids."

But when you consistently ignore your inner voice—the one that reminds you to be kind to your partner, patient with your children, and honest about what you really feel—what you have to say to your family may very well cause a breakdown in communication at the very least. At worst, you may already be at odds with each other and feel that your way back to good communication may be an impossible journey. The good news is that it's not impossible. It simply requires a commitment to begin communicating compassionately and the ability to forgive each other for the hurts that have been accumulating along the way.

Master the Art of Assertive Communication

To communicate assertively requires a conscious effort on your part. It's all too common for people who share their daily lives to make assumptions about what the other is thinking, to assume that because you've known your partner for X number of years, you can speak for him. It can feel awkward to begin the process of using "I feel" statements. In fact, at first you might even be embarrassed. After all, many of us were raised by a generation of parents whose attitude was "Who cares what you feel? Just do it." Yet it's important that a nonthreatening climate be established to encourage meaningful dialogue. Nonverbal cues are also an important part of assertive communication. Making direct eye contact, listening attentively, sitting in a relaxed manner, and nodding at appropriate moments—all of these behaviors convey a message that you're a respectful, attentive, and open-minded listener.

Too many discussions begin with a negative statement, like "We really have a problem" or "How could you have done that?" This approach immediately puts the other person on the defensive and serves only to heighten a confrontation. Using "I" messages is much more effective, as in "I need to have more time to myself" or "I felt hurt that you didn't call to tell me you'd be late for dinner." With "I" messages you accept ownership of your own feelings. Also important here is affirming and validating feelings of your partner as well. This sets the stage for candid dialogue.

Here are some positive statements that are useful for introducing subjects that could lead to discord:

- "It seems to me we've been distant, but I want us to be closer."
- "Because I want you to understand me, I would like to talk with you."
- "Although this issue is difficult to talk about, I'm raising it because I value you and our relationship."
- "I love you, and I want to tell you how I feel."
- "I want to understand your point of view, so let's talk."

Along with introducing a sensitive subject tactfully, assertive communication involves listening without getting defensive, which can be hard to do when your initial response is anger with your partner. Let's say you come home from work and the children's toys are spread out like carpeting across the living room floor. Meanwhile, your partner is watching TV as he lounges in a recliner. If you say, "Are you on vacation?," what you may really mean is that you're unhappy to come home to a mess that you feel he had time to deal with. This sarcastic statement is a passive-aggressive one. And your partner may very well respond, "Look, the kids ran me ragged all day. I just needed five minutes to myself. Besides, it's only toys. Don't get in a dither." His comments are born out of a need to defend himself against what he views as your attack. And we all know that this conversation could be headed toward a heated argument that never really addresses some basic issues, such as that both parents are tired. One didn't want to come home to see yet another thing she has to take care of. The other needed time to unwind, and then would likely have gotten to the straightening of the toys—or better yet, gotten the children involved.

With a little effort, however, an argument needn't be inevitable. Your partner might listen carefully to your comment and say, "It sounds like you had a hard day at work. It must be disappointing to you to see the mess." This shows he's trying to be attentive and respectful of your feelings. Your response might then be, "Yes, I did, and I'm sorry I took it out on you. I know the kids can be tiring, too. Let's get the kids in here and have a cleanup party after dinner." Together you've turned a defensive conversation into an assertive, compassionate one.

Sometimes you may need to increase your level of assertiveness. If it becomes a pattern that your partner lets the children leave a mess behind when they play, so that you're always the one who has to initiate a cleanup brigade, you might first say, "It disturbs me that you're not enforcing our household rule that we all clean up after ourselves." If that doesn't work, try, "I don't think you realize how strongly I feel about this. Please support me on this issue with the kids." Finally, if you're still not making headway, you might say, "It's vital to me that we resolve this issue. I would like us to get some outside help."

And always remember that you have basic human rights. When you feel those rights may be threatened, reaffirm them by repeating these statements (adapted from Robert Alberti's "Bill of Assertive Rights") to yourself:

- I have the right to my own opinion.
- I have the right to be treated with respect.
- I have the right to change my mind.
- I have the right to say no.
- I have the right to pursue happiness.
- I have the right to make mistakes and be responsible for them.
- I have the right to say I don't understand.

Even with assertive communication, you'll have times when you find yourself slipping into communication pitfalls. These moments when you grasp at old patterns because you're too tired or haven't thought it through are just plain human. Fortunately, there are ways to avoid or overcome pitfalls.

1. *Be prepared for pitfalls and recognize that they're inevitable.*
    There is no perfectly harmonious communication in family life. Self-reflection and awareness will help you to understand your negative patterns and your partner's weak spots. If you frequently become defensive when you're given constructive criticism, try these techniques to avoid becoming defensive:

    - Count to ten.
    - Take deep breaths, imagining yourself as a peacemaker.
    - Commit to listening, and don't respond until you reflect and validate.
    - If you know you're overly critical, make positive statements first. Acknowledge what's going well first.
    - Ask for what you want changed in a positive way. For example, "I like it when you come home on time. It makes me feel safe and appreciated" instead of "I hate it when you're late."

2. *Practice, practice, practice communicating compassionately.*

3. *Apologize and forgive—and try again when you don't get it right.*

4. *Make time to talk.* Sometimes it's not your communication style that's putting a cramp in your communication as partners and parents. The culprit may be your lack of time together. If you're like most modern families, you and your partner divvy up the carpooling duties, with you taking your daughter to soccer while your partner takes your son to his karate class. Later that day you might all be together, but the children want your respective attentions, to tell you about their respective afternoons. When you finally get them to

bed and have a quiet moment alone together . . . well, it's not surprising that rather than deep, compassionate communication, what you may be sharing are loud, tired snores on the couch.

Yet couples need time to talk to one another without interruption from children. Yes, your children need times when they have your undivided attention, and scheduling these times is essential. But in order to communicate with one another in ways that will benefit your whole family, you need to speak about more than whose turn it is to take out the garbage.

Often we get lost in the day-to-day and forget that before we were ever parents, we were two people who shared a life together, with hopes and dreams. Hold on to that memory.

Seven Golden Rules of Communication

Sometimes what you say matters less than how you say it. When it comes to communicating compassionately with your partner—and children—we recommend that you follow the seven golden rules of communication. These are:

1. *Initiate dialogue.* Although it may seem easier to ignore conflicts than try to resolve them, wounds left to fester never heal properly and will eventually undermine your family stability. Hold fast to your vision of yourself as a peacemaker, someone who is eager to reach a level of understanding. Choose the appropriate time and place in which to start difficult conversations.

2. *Listen actively.* Use both verbal and nonverbal signals to let your partner know that you're focusing undivided attention on what he has to say. Repeating his words—"You're saying you'd like me to help you more with carpooling the kids around"—is one way to underscore your attentiveness and encourage him to volunteer more information. Asking open-ended questions that cannot be answered

with a simple yes or no also lets him know that you really want to understand what's bothering him. An example: Rather than asking, "Do you have everything under control?" you can express a greater willingness to help by saying, "How can I help you?"

3. *Validate feelings.* Your partner's genuine emotional responses deserve respect. Feelings are never right or wrong; they simply reflect a person's subjective experience. If she says, "I feel as though I'm making all the decisions with the kids," it's unfair to say, "You're being ridiculous!" Allow her to own her feelings. Support her by saying, "You're telling me you want me to offer you more support."

4. *Don't interrupt.* While your partner is expressing her point of view, limit your comments and questions to what's needed for purposes of clarification. Otherwise, the message you send says, "What you have to say is not as important as what I have to say." Your turn to offer a more detailed response will come later.

5. *Stay on the subject.* Don't drag other grievances or old hurts into current conversation. Resolve one conflict at a time.

6. *Fight fair.* No matter how angry you feel, never deliberately hurt your partner. There's nothing more destructive than focusing on his vulnerable spots or making nasty comments about something you know he's sensitive about. Long after an argument is resolved, the raw wounds inflicted by those cruel words will linger. Speak carefully, and don't go on the defensive.

7. *Respect differences.* No matter how articulately you state your position, you may not be able to convince your partner to see things that way. Sometimes a conflict can be resolved only by an agreement to disagree.

Following these rules is the compassionate approach to communication. Moreover, when you practice this method of interaction, you're modeling a valuable tool for your children.

What Your Children Are Telling You

As difficult as it may be to communicate with your partner from time to time, you may find that your communication with your children is harder. When your children feel that you don't listen to them or understand what they say, eventually they stop talking to you. Obviously, that's not something you want. Children who feel they can't communicate with their parents often turn to outside influences that may have a negative impact on their choices, or they may withdraw inward and in silent anguish adopt self-destructive behaviors.

Just as you can't communicate with your partner perfectly all the time, the way in which you communicate with your children will also be influenced by how stressed you are, by how much time you all have together, and by their moods as well. Still, as you've done with the previous two Principles, it's helpful to gauge where you and your partner stand when it comes to truly listening and responding to your children. Answer *Yes* or *No* to the following questions:

1. Do you find that you have little time to sit and talk with your children without other distractions or activities?

2. Do you plan activities and events without talking to your children ahead of time?

3. Do you initiate dialogue with your children after school?

4. Do you listen attentively when your children talk and try to reflect or paraphrase what was said?

5. Do you validate your children's feelings by verbalizing understanding of how they feel? Even when you must follow through with discipline or setting limits?

6. Do you get impatient and rush your children to get to the point when they're talking?

7. Do you compare your children to their siblings or to other children?

8. Do you engage in destructive communication such as name-calling or saying things like "Shut up" or "You can be so stupid"?

9. Have there been times when your child was reluctant to tell you what was on her mind?

10. Does your child often show conflicting feelings about what's bothering him?

If you answered yes to questions 1, 2, 6, 7, 8, 9, or 10 or no to questions 3, 4, or 5, there are areas of your communication with your children that can be improved.

Typically, a child will communicate through his behavior. For example, if a child frequently provokes other children, he's saying something about what he feels. Children don't always know how to put feelings into words. So they act the way they feel. They slam their bedroom doors even as they insist nothing is wrong. With children, in order to better understand their feelings, parents always have to take into account not only what they say, but also what they do.

If Dan says he likes to play only with Charlie, he's obviously telling you something about how he feels about this friend. But what else is going on? Does he make this statement because other kids have rejected him? Or is it a more positive situation, in that he simply genuinely likes Charlie? How you answer these questions will depend on how well you know your child's verbal and behavioral cues. Facial expressions, gestures, and tone of voice all reveal feelings. Hugs, smiles, anger, and tantrums provide other clues as to what a child may be feeling. So in the case of Dan, if he says he likes to play only with Charlie and his facial expression and tone of voice reflect sadness, there's your cue to ask for more details. But if he smiles and hugs you as he prances off to make plans for his playdate with Charlie, you can probably rest assured your child is quite happy about his friendship with the boy.

Now, this may seem fairly basic and obvious, but to carry out this exercise requires time and observation on your part. The first step in communicating compassionately with your children is observing their behavior and understanding the feelings behind it. You can always improve communication with your children by finding out what they're feeling. Of course, children, like adults, can express a wide range of feelings in their behavior, and more than one at a time. If your son comes home feeling angry that his teacher criticized him in front of the class, what else might he be feeling? He might be recalling his embarrassment and surprise at being singled out, and he might feel guilt at his wrongdoing. Allowing him the time and space in which to express all the feelings he has is an important role you must assume.

Family Communication Skills

Good communication skills are learned. We're not born with them. And these skills will be refined throughout our lives. We're taught by our families, our teachers, our friends, and by our culture at large. And we teach children the skills of communication mostly by how we model those skills. It's important to allow your children to express their views, feelings, and ideas. Yet that's not always what happens. Let's take a look at some of the skills that are essential for talking and listening to children.

1. *Always listen actively.* Children love to chatter and give you lots of details until your eyes glaze over. Take Linda's situation, for example.

Tara came running in from school excited about an upcoming play. As she began to tell Linda, Linda was trying to finish up a term paper for a course she was taking at community college. She said, "Oh, that's so nice, baby. That's really good. There's a snack for you on the table, and then please start your homework." Later that night Linda was up putting the finishing touches on her paper when she realized that she hadn't even asked Tara what the play was about, how she felt about the play, or what part she wanted. Linda wanted to wake Tara up and apologize.

How often have you realized, five minutes after your child speaks to you, that you haven't really listened?

Listening actively helps your child develop confidence in self-expression. Your attention validates her feelings and enhances her self-esteem. And your children expect you to listen. After all, you expect them to listen to you, but parents don't always extend them the same courtesy. Further, when you listen to dialogue that seems to have little meaning to you, your ears will be able to perk up when there is something you need to hear about. There is always at least one important thought or observation and a feeling in their conversation with you. A child's dialogue is often like an oyster hiding a pearl. Sometimes hidden inside the words about what she ate for lunch and who looked at whom on the playground are the gems revealing how upset she was that her usual seat in the cafeteria was taken by her best friend's newest confidante.

When we listen to our children, we also teach them we respect them. We may not allow them to engage in a particular activity, but we can listen and let them know that we understand their disappointment. For example, we could say, "Jenny, I know that you really want to go to the movies with your friends and that you're disappointed, but we have a busy schedule today, and you may not go." Just remember that when listening, you need to make time for the conversation. Avoid hurrying her through the discussion; otherwise, she'll feel unnecessary pressure and ease of communication will be lost.

Active listening is simple to do, produces immediate results, and can be revealing to both you and your child. There are four simple steps to good listening:

- Restate your child's remarks to make sure you're hearing them correctly and to let her know you're listening. (Not unlike what we've already told you to do with your partner.)

- Ask open-ended questions to clarify the situation further.

- State your understanding of the problem.

- Withhold judgment until you have all the facts.

2. *Give open responses.* The way you respond to your children also determines how much information you get from them. There are two types of responses you could give when your child asks you a question: open and closed. Closed responses tend to shut off communication, while open responses encourage it. Say your daughter asks you if you ever told a lie as a child and you respond, "I don't think that's something you should be asking me," you've just shut down communication. You've also lost a wonderful teaching moment, an opportunity to give your child the information she so clearly craves in order to direct her own life. In this case, a good open response would be "Yes I did. I didn't want to get into trouble for breaking Grandma's vase, so I lied and said the neighbor's boy did it. But Grandma found out the truth. I'll never forget the look on Grandma's face when she learned I had lied. I knew I had disappointed her, and that was far more painful to her than the loss of her vase. I hope you know that I'll always listen to what you have to say,

even if I don't always like what I hear. I'd rather you tell me the truth and we'll deal with the consequences together than to learn you felt there was something you couldn't tell me." Open responses are an integral part of good communication skills, and they're helpful in keeping a flow of dialogue.

3. *Use "I" statements instead of "you" statements.* A child who is involved in a conflict might be wrestling with feelings of anger, frustration, sadness, regret, fear, or anxiety. While none of us feel good with these emotions churning inside us, it's not unusual for a person to assign responsibility for them to others. People who see others as responsible for their feelings tend to describe their conflicts in terms of "you" messages. A typical response for a child upset about an argument with a sibling might be "You always take her side. You let her go in my room."

For our children's emotional well-being as well as for the development of their communication skills, it's important to teach them "I" statements instead, similar to the "I feel" statements we encourage you to use with your partner. Children tend to react to conflict in automatic ways because they forget, or don't know, that they have choices in the ways they respond. Encouraging your children to use "I" statements is a way to teach them they're responsible for the way they feel in different situations and that by controlling their feelings they can choose their reactions.

Getting children to speak this way can be difficult at first. But you can encourage them to begin all statements with the word "I": "I feel like you don't care about my stuff when you don't tell Sue to stay out of my room."

4. *Respect children's privacy.* When your children face crises, you're naturally anxious to see them resolve these crises. At times you may press them for explanations they're not prepared to give. It's always a mistake to force your child to express her feelings. A better

approach is to listen to whatever she has to say at the time and gradually encourage her to express herself further.

If you invade your child's privacy by forcing her to speak against her will, it could take a lot of work to undo the damage. A good rule to follow is to look for those nonverbal cues we mentioned to determine what she's feeling. Then just remind her you're there to listen if she wants to talk.

Another aspect of respecting children's privacy is for parents to remember not to be so quick to solve their children's problems for them, rather than letting them work them out themselves. For instance, Samantha comes home from playing and she's crying. Her friend Jill told her that she wasn't her friend anymore. Tim, Samantha's father, says, "Don't worry. It'll be okay. You have lots of other friends. Why don't you go call Donna?" Samantha sobs and replies, "I don't want another friend. I want Jill to be my friend. I hate myself. Nobody likes me."

Sometimes we want to offer solutions without asking our children if they can work out a problem themselves. We have to try to let them problem-solve on their own, listen, validate their feelings, and support and guide (if necessary) their solutions. Another approach would be to say, "You seem upset by what Jill said. Let's talk about it. What would you like to do about this situation?" Sometimes they'll need your help with brainstorming for solutions.

5. *Respect children's feelings.* In relating to our children, we sometimes forget that as people they deserve the same respect we want for ourselves and give to other people. Think of how we behave when we're angry or upset. Often we just want to be left alone. Isn't it fair to assume that our children might want the same thing?

But many people have been taught that feelings of anger, disappointment, or fear are wrong and shouldn't be expressed, so we don't always know how to handle these feelings when our children express them. We may take on familiar roles, at times being the person in charge, demanding that our child gets rid of the feelings, as in "Stop that now." At other times we lecture and advise, strutting our superior problem-solving skills. Sometimes we preach what they should and shouldn't do. But many times all they really want is a sympathetic listener.

If we're understanding and sensitive to how our children feel, they'll reward us with their trust. Prying information out of them and trying to solve their problems before we understand them will alienate them. A better approach is to allow children to experience their feelings and tell us about them when they feel they understand them or when they ask for our help.

Even when you're sure you understand what your child is really feeling, one important step remains. It's a simple one that we often overlook. Ask them if there is anything you can help with rather than telling them what to do.

And one final point about respect: Don't criticize your child, and don't name-call. Both will be damaging not only to the conversation of the moment but to your relationship of a lifetime.

Teaching Children to Listen

It's important to teach children active listening skills. Children learn to listen naturally over time if you use active listening skills yourself. But you can reinforce them along the way by having your child repeat back what you've said. The way you do so will depend on your child's developmental stage, however.

With a preschool child, if you say, "Denny, don't run," your child thinks you mean for the rest of his life. Try to be concise but clear. For example, you can say, "Denny, please walk carefully. Don't run on the tile floor. I feel nervous, because you may slip, and I don't want you to get hurt." Then have your child repeat back what you said.

With a grade-school child, have her repeat back what you said, but also seek continued dialogue to encourage and teach open communication. This will instill respect for your authority but also begin the process of negotiation and compromise. For example, "The rule is that you may watch PG movies. Why do you want to watch a movie that is PG-13?"

With adolescents, allow for more freedom of expression and compromise. However, the limits and boundaries that are nonnegotiable should be clear and firm. At this age, the way to help your child listen is to follow five steps:

- Show empathy. "I know you really want to watch the movie."

- Be clear. "You may not watch R-rated movies at thirteen years old."

- Encourage dialogue. "Why did you want to watch it? What have you heard about it?"

- Restate your position. "I can understand how you feel; however, we told you our rule."

- Compromise when your child's age and the issue are appropriate.

Encouraging Compassionate Communication

How often do you give your children the message that they are valued? That is the core message that should come through all of your communication.

Children want to be sure you love them. You can't validate them every moment, but at critical moments always stop and give a hug. Express your love when your child needs it—as well as when you want to share it.

The most important aspect of encouraging compassionate communication in your family is setting aside enough time for it to happen. Here are some suggestions that will help:

- Sit down to dinner together often during the week.

- Hold a weekly family meeting that allows children the opportunity to share their feelings about family matters, schedules, activities, school, friends, and so on. These meetings offer opportunities to practice communication skills. They demonstrate that building communication is a priority in your family.

- When you tuck your children into bed at night, allow the extra moments they need to speak with you, even if the clock ticks past their bedtime.

- Show your children that you care about them. This may require stopping for a moment and asking yourself, "What would make my child or partner feel valued?"

- Listen to, reflect, and validate their feelings, even if you don't agree with their perception. Then state your point of view assertively.

- Make honest communication a goal, even when it is uncomfortable.

We realize that communication after a divorce can be a particular challenge, especially if your split was hostile rather than congenial. To have to speak to someone because of the child you share, when you've chosen for one reason or other to put this person out of your life, can be very painful. Initially, many divorced parents wish they didn't have to communicate at all anymore.

However, effective communication between parents becomes even more essential after a divorce. Your children will need teamwork from you in order to adjust to the new lifestyle. To let them observe you treat each other with compassion and respect is one of the greatest gifts you can offer your children. It will shape their view of the world and affect their emotional development. There will be functions like school plays, sports events, family affairs, and birthday parties where you will both be present. This will create some fear and anxiety for your children. Your attitude, behavior, and interaction will either increase or decrease this fear. Always remember that you want to do what is in their best interests.

Sometimes couples need mediation. In any case, you must at least try to understand how your children view divorce and how your interaction with one another affects their sense of security. Young children can't always express themselves in words. They're not emotionally mature enough. However, their behavior and attitudes will often reflect what they're feeling. Encourage your children to share their feelings with you. How? Make the time to sit down and play together. Activities such as playing with dolls and toys, coloring and drawing, writing and keeping journals help children express their innermost thoughts.

Living the Third Principle

Your desire for team spirit shows as you respect each individual's feelings. You want to feel worthwhile and cared about. You want your child and your partner in parenting to feel valued, too.

Ideally, by routinely communicating with compassion for their feelings, you are teaching them to reciprocate. But you and your partner have to walk the walk, not just talk the talk.

Walking the walk includes being able to apologize and admit your mistakes, especially when you "lose it." It's okay to show and discuss that you're not perfect as a parent or partner, but it's essential to own up to your feelings and demonstrate a better way. If you're under stress and you happen to yell or communicate in a negative manner, apologize and then verbalize your displeasure in a more caring manner.

4

Reach Out to Your Village: The Fourth Principle

My village provides the additional support my team needs to thrive. I will honor these team members and be available to work harmoniously with them.

The Team Beyond Your Doorstep

The good times of parenting—your child's first steps, words, lost tooth, school play, and even those first heartwarming smiles and tender kisses— you're probably happy and proud to share with anyone who will listen. The more difficult moments may be ones you keep to yourself. You may feel that no one wants to be "burdened" with your small problem. Or that your child's poor behavior is too embarrassing to share. Or that no one else has ever experienced this, so no one would understand. Or that you don't air dirty laundry. Or that you should be able to work this out on your own. Or that you're too proud to ask for help.

The truth is, though, that your world is probably brimming with people who would be happy to lend a hand or a friendly ear. From extended family members to community members to people in your place of worship, your child's school, and your work, there is an entire constellation of support waiting to help you as soon as you ask.

In fact, several people in your child's life are probably already providing guidance and direction. A teacher may instill values of perseverance, determination, and discipline. A coach may provide structure and teach self-control. A doctor may diagnose a special condition. There are many people who are willing and available to assist you with your child. Determining who and what you need for support is the task at hand.

When Sandy and Eric disapproved of their fifteen-year-old daughter's boyfriend, it just seemed to make her interest in him grow stronger.

The guy had dropped out of high school and was known as a troublemaker in the community. Carla seemed to think she could change him and that her inspiration would help him do better. Sandy was beside herself with worry about Carla's becoming sexually active. Eric couldn't stand the sight of her boyfriend. Their home front had become a battleground of wills where there could be no winners, because everyone was being wounded.

It was Eric's sister Tina who came to the rescue. She was visiting for a holiday and witnessed a tension-filled exchange between Eric, Sandy, and Carla. During Tina's visit she spoke first to Eric and Sandy and then to Carla to hear their differing points of view. Then, acting as a loving family member and mediator, Tina encouraged Sandy and Eric at least to interact with Carla's boyfriend in order to make a fair judgment. She told them this would show Carla that they were trying to understand and consider a compromise instead of being rigid and controlling. It was clear that Carla was sneaking around to see her boyfriend, and this was leading to major confrontations. Carla needed to respect her parents' authority and rules. However, she needed her parents to be more flexible.

Tina's support helped the family to communicate more effectively. In time Carla recognized that she didn't have enough in common with her boyfriend. In addition, he did go back to school after spending time with Sandy, Eric, and Tina. The truth was, although they didn't want Carla to date him seriously, they had become fond of him.

But it took an "outsider" to assess the situation. Though Tina loved all parties involved, as an extended family member who did not live with them and did not have any agenda, she was able to evaluate the situation with an uncluttered view. In so doing, she was able to provide the family with some much-needed support.

You, too, will encounter times in your lifelong parenting career when you'll need support from someone other than your partner. Perhaps you already have that support in place, though you might not be taking advantage of as many different aspects of it as you could. Take this inventory to find out. Answer *Yes* or *No* to the following questions.

1. Can you depend on extended family members to give you support?
2. Do you have friends to encourage and assist you when needed?
3. Does a religious leader provide inspiration and guidance for you?

4. Does your child's school work with you as a team in educating your child?

5. Is there a coach, music teacher, dance instructor, or someone else who influences your child in a positive way?

6. Do you have paid support people who help you (baby-sitter, nanny)?

7. Do you have difficulty asking for help when you feel over-whelmed with the number of things you must handle?

8. Do you feel alone and unable to depend on others for support?

If you answered yes to questions 1 through 6 and no to questions 7 and 8, then you have the support you need and are able to rely on others appropriately. However, if you answered no to questions 1 through 6 and yes to 7 or 8, then that is an area that needs girding.

How to Ask for Help

Pride, embarrassment, and fear are all feelings that can inhibit us. But growing a loving family includes being able to identify problems and seek solutions. It takes strength and courage to reach out to others. Team-spirited parents realize that a support system doesn't take anything away from them or reflect negatively on them. To the contrary, it allows for increased family intimacy, greater understanding, and improved relationships.

But maybe you don't know how to ask for help. Maybe you were raised to be independent, with the notion that asking for help is a sign of weakness. Fortunately, asking for help is easy, once you get beyond your hesitation. Here's our step-by-step guide to asking for help:

1. *Acknowledge that you have difficulty asking for help.*

2. *Identify the person you would most like to receive support from.*

3. *Determine if you feel most comfortable writing, calling, or talking face to face.*

4. *Prepare a written statement.* For example, "I have some difficulty talking about this, but I would really like to be able to have you help me with a situation."

5. *Clearly state what you need.* For example, to be able to talk through a problem; help with after-school transportation, cooking lessons, or meal preparation; company at a child's sporting event, etc.

6. *Express understanding.* For example, "If you're not able to do this, I understand."

7. *Consider other support alternatives and try again.*

When to Seek Professional Help for Yourself

Sometimes you need an objective person to provide guidance and support. Family members might be too close to the situation and too emotionally involved to be constructive. But you may be unsure whether you need outside help. To guide you in making that decision, here's a checklist:

You can tell that you need professional help for yourself if:

- You feel overwhelmed and unable to cope (manifested by being immobilized and having difficulty functioning).

- You act impatient and irritable (manifested possibly by lashing out at your children and overreacting).

- You're withdrawn and feel hopeless about parenting (manifested by isolating yourself and not intervening with your children or guiding them).

- You feel anxious, insecure, and helpless (manifested in an inability to follow through or make decisions).

If you need to seek help for yourself, check with your family practitioner first, and ask for referrals from friends and family if you feel comfortable doing so. Keep in mind that the longer you wait to deal with these issues, the more they can consume your own and your family's emotional health.

When to Seek Professional Help for Your Child

You can tell that you need professional help for your child if:

- She experiences a sudden change in behavior or personality.
- His behavior is uncharacteristic and persists for an extended time.
- She creates conflict and problems for other family members that can no longer be ignored or tolerated.
- He has inappropriate or excessive emotional expression, including anger, sadness, disappointment, resentment, or fears.

If you need to seek professional help for your child, ask for a recommendation from your child's pediatrician or the school psychologist. These people can provide expert advice and, if necessary, can refer you to other professionals who can assist you further.

How Family Therapy Can Help

Family therapy may be one option for your team. In family therapy, family members can focus on their problems and conflicts in a safe environment with a neutral and objective professional. The goal of family therapy is to become more aware of the issues and improve the communication among family members. This includes learning new approaches to resolving conflicts and solving problems. Family members gain insight into how they interact and communicate in certain patterns that interfere with having healthy relationships.

Family therapists cover a range of professionals with varying backgrounds and areas of expertise. A local mental health agency is likely to have trained and skilled professionals in counseling, social work, psychology, and psychiatry. A master's-level counselor is certified and able to support you in addressing marital and family issues. A master's-level clinical social worker is also trained in mental health and can address family, individual, and marital issues. A doctorate-level psychologist conducts therapy and also administers psychological evaluations and testing. A psychiatrist is a medical doctor who provides psychotherapy and can also evaluate a patient for and prescribe medication.

There is no shame in seeking professional help. And depending on the nature of your situation, it can even be a short-term stop along your parenting journey.

Rediscover Your Village

In a society in which people move around more than ever and must cope with the consequences of separation and divorce, uplifting interaction with others has become more important—and more challenging—than ever.

At one time families could count on the support of grandparents who lived around the corner and siblings who lived just the next town over. Today more families than not, because of careers that have taken them far from their hometowns, live hundreds of miles from their extended family members. Once mothers and fathers could chat with their neighbors over the backyard fence. Now most neighbors spend their weekdays working and their weekends running errands. Many families don't even know their neighbors, though they may have lived next door to one another for years. Community members, too, may be unknown to you as huge chains swallow small neighborhood stores, though there was a time when you could walk into a store and everyone there knew your name. And people who once derived much support and inspiration from their religious leaders may find themselves making the choice to stay home and read the paper rather than attend religious services on their one day to relax.

But all that can change, with a little ingenuity on your part. The first step is to open the arms of your family to let your needs be known and allow the support of others. The rest of this chapter is all about how to do that.

For example, there are times when the two of us need to travel for workshops, book signings, or speaking engagements. It's difficult to leave our children, and we don't want to burden others. We're most comfortable having Darlene's parents care for our children. Our children spend a great deal of time with them, and because they have retired, they have flexible schedules. They travel a great deal and are loving enough to schedule their vacations around our work schedules. Darlene's friend, Pam, who is like the big sister Darlene never had, also arranges her schedule to help out.

There are times when we feel it may be an imposition, but we share our feelings, ask for the help we need, and show our appreciation. Of course, there is no one, no matter how well intentioned they are, who can raise and care for your children as you can. For instance, we don't allow our children to watch much television, but Nana and Granddaddy do. Although there is some difference in values, we have to be flexible and open. Reaching a compromise requires communicating and respecting each other's views. Auntie Pam *insists* that they eat vegetables, and we only *encourage* our children to do so. This, too, requires open communication and understanding.

We've had to come to terms with the fact that, like most grandparents, Nana and Granddaddy just want to relax with our children and have fun with them. They don't want to worry unduly about the process we enforce. So even if the children watch TV, we know that their emotional and physical well-being won't be compromised. All it takes is for us to get them back on schedule when they come home.

And even if Auntie Pam is more structured than we are, we know that our children will be fine in her care. After all, vegetables never hurt anyone.

In short, our village includes many people who share our concerns and core values. All the people in our village do not share all of our values, and that's okay. Of course, we have limits.

What does that mean for you? Maybe you don't like people smoking around your children. Is that the only thing causing you to hold back in asking your sister's help? Perhaps you can ask your sister not to smoke indoors when your children are there. If she refuses, you have to decide how flexible you can be.

Keep in mind, too, that while you may have issues with a helper, you should not pass your issues on to your child. Unless you fear for your child's emotional or physical safety, remember that members of your village share a special bond with your child, one not mired in issues that may have affected you. This applies to any family member, friend, or community member whom you call an important member of your village.

Another thing you should watch out for is managing your own prejudices without passing them on to your children. If you had experiences in the past with a certain ethnic group—say, you're white and a black child stole your books in sixth grade, or you're black and a white child stole your books—you don't want to project to your children a belief that all black/white people are thieves. Try not to generalize and stereotype any group. Instead, determine where your bias is coming from and work through it for your own sake, as well as your child's. If your child's soccer coach is Latino and this triggers some past anxiety for you, you need to see the person who is in front of you, not your past experiences. You don't want to limit your child's opportunities because someone is different from you.

Reach Out to Extended Family Members

With extended family members there will typically be history and shared experiences that inspire both loving and uncomfortable feelings for you. Knowing their background and values helps to determine in what areas you can seek their support. If Aunt Sally doesn't like dogs and you remember the time she hit your dog with the newspaper, you certainly wouldn't ask her to feed your son's cocker spaniel when you were out of town.

The relationship that the generations share is another unique and powerful bond. Reaching out to grandparents will serve your children well throughout their lives—and may even help to lessen whatever bitterness lies between you and your parents. (Though of course that's not your child's responsibility.)

The value of extended family members is golden. Through a network of kinship ties, you gain role models for your children, sources of emotional or financial support, and dependable allies in a sometimes-frightening world. You also get the chance to tap in to the better values and experiences you recalled in Principle One. The aunt who instilled your love of reading can now share that with your daughter. Your brother who started his own business can take your son to work to show him the result of believing in your dreams. Family members can stand by your side in good times to celebrate and in bad times to lend support. Particularly if you're a single parent, another family member may very well become a key member of your parenting team.

Reach Out to Friends

We get to choose our friends, unlike our family members. And also unlike with family, we typically feel less demand or pressure to put up with ongoing problems with a friend. We don't have to. So, often our friends are people we have purposely selected as dependable, trustworthy, and caring. If not, it is time to reevaluate the friendship. Offering and receiving support should be reciprocal.

A friend can be another member of your village who is able to provide a source of stimulating ideas, insights, and even friendly tips about matters of parenting issues. Chances are that friend will have children around the ages of your own and can be a sounding board about the more serious as well as the lighter moments of parenting. Your friend can be your confidant about the aspects of parenting that make you feel insecure. And a friend can offer a welcome break in your routine when you and your partner need to get away for an evening or a weekend.

Reach Out to Your Community

With community members like neighbors and store owners, we tend to need to be the most selective and exercise appropriate boundaries. A church member whom you have gotten to know well could baby-sit on occasion. A retired teacher could tutor your son in math. A coach could talk to your daughter about keeping up her grades. These people can become as important to your family life as you let them be.

Your participation in community life is good for your whole family. Find programs or events that need volunteers in order to increase your community connections and involvement. Visit nursing homes or day care centers, the sick and shut-in from your church. Have your child interact with a child you're mentoring or tutoring. Attend cultural events. All of these broaden your child's world as well as your own.

When asked how much support people get from their community and how involved they are in their community, many people today shake their heads as though the idea never occurred to them. Yet research indicates that when you participate in your community, you derive many psychological benefits. When you are involved in and committed to a community project, for instance, you have the sense that you are an active director in your life, rather than a passive victim of the world around you. It decreases your sense of isolation and powerlessness and increases your feelings of self-respect.

When you take action in your community, you draw on your compassion, energy and pride. By concentrating on goals that go beyond your front door, you enhance your sense of humanity in your community and see yourself as a contributor to society. Neighborhood groups have fought successfully to ban the building of nuclear testing sites. They've worked together to help less-fortunate community members. Community groups have revitalized decaying neighborhoods, and playgrounds have been built for community children. Other groups have forced politicians to look at such issues as increased incidence of breast cancer in their communities and a whole host of other political issues. Neighbors and community members have been able to pull together on a smaller scale as well, pooling their resources to lend support to others in times of need.

The point is that by working together, neighbors and community groups do create a village, one in which the members care for each other. Although there is a strong "not in my backyard" sentiment in this country, when people work together, this destructive philosophy falls on its face. When you work with others, you feel more whole, more connected to the world, and less consumed by your daily troubles and projects. That's not a feeling that, once gained, you'll likely let go of again. Our children benefit when they see and experience our involvement. For one thing, they know where to turn. That neighbor down the block who was once a stranger can now be identified as a safe person should the children in the community be out playing one day and need help. Seeing you as part of a community also gives children a sense of belonging to a larger picture. They realize all the benefits you do, but they also gain the roots you most likely had as a child growing up in different times. There is a comfort in walking into a store and having the owner greet you by name, setting aside the comic book she knows you'll be looking for. This consideration gives children a feeling of self-worth, a sense that someone else values who they are. And when they participate in community-improvement events and help you stuff envelopes for a cause, they learn that they are getting a glimpse of responsible adulthood.

If reaching out to your neighbors and community seems awkward to you, take another look at the guidelines for "How to Ask for Help" on page 80.

Reach Out to Your Religious Leader

We've spoken about the need to seek outside professional help when times overwhelm you. Your religious leader can be a source of comfort and strength in both good times and trying times. Yet for many people this is the last person to whom they turn. You may feel guilty because you haven't attended services regularly. You may have some religious baggage that you haven't yet dealt with. But the basic religious belief is to go to God just as you are. In fact, most religious organizations are clear that people come to them in need. Most people wouldn't attend a place of worship if they didn't believe they had room to grow spiritually.

Churches, synagogues, and other houses of worship can provide spiritual guidance and support. Typically, you will be welcomed and encouraged to participate in prayer. There are usually programs for children and parenting support services. You need not feel pressured to join. Be open about your need to learn more about the teachings and practices of the church and acknowledge your desire for support in raising your children to be spiritually strong. Most religious leaders will be happy to make an appointment with you to discuss any or all of these issues.

Reach Out to Your Child's School

From the time she starts full-time school, around kindergarten, your child spends the better part of her day under the care of the members of her school's faculty and staff. As she rises through the grades, that time spent in school increases, thanks to after-school and extracurricular activities. By the time she's in high school, what with homework, activities, and her ever-increasing social life, you might just begin to feel that you and your child are like two ships passing in the night. But it doesn't need to be like that. In fact, for your child's academic success, it *shouldn't* be like that.

Because your child's teachers and school staff share so much of her day and exercise a good deal of influence over your child, you are all partners in parenting.

Do you and the school staff work together? Take a moment for assessment.

1. Did you visit your child's school prior to your child's enrollment, and do you continue to be present regularly?

2. Do you know your child's teacher?

3. Have you met the special teachers and support staff?

4. Have you met the school principal?

5. Are you aware of who is on your local school board and who your superintendent is? Are you an informed voter in school district elections?

6. Do you network with other parents?

7. Are you familiar with school policies relating to tardiness, discipline, and other school rules?

8. Do you keep track of new developments at school?

9. Are you aware of what your child will be learning and expected to know this year?

10. Have you or your partner volunteered in the classroom or on field trips and attended school activities?

11. Do you and your partner address problems about your child's education together?

Obviously we think the answer to *all* these questions should be yes for each partner. To utilize fully the support you can get for your child from the educational environment, you need to be involved. That doesn't mean you need to be up at the school daily, or be on first-name terms with the principal, or use all your sick days to chaperone class trips. But it does mean that you should do your own homework so to ensure that you know who is educating your child and how you can work together.

There are some very basic steps we recommend you take once your child begins his school career. Divorced partners can follow these steps independently.

1. *Meet with your child's teacher.* School districts ordinarily schedule parent-teacher conferences at the end of the first marking period. Because teachers must meet with about twenty parents over the course of three afternoons, their time with you is limited. Teachers rarely have time for an in-depth discussion of your child during these conferences. Meanwhile, the first weeks of school have passed, and your child may already have adopted some poor work habits or be having some real difficulties.

Parents have a right to schedule get-acquainted conferences earlier in the school year. If your child has special issues that she has been struggling with in prior grades, or if something happened in your family life during the summer, your child's new teacher needs to know this.

We can't emphasize enough that the more ongoing communication you have with the teacher, the better chances your child has for a successful year. Teachers want to help your child. When you help a teacher get to know your child better, he or she has an immediate opportunity to be prepared for the best way to work with your child during the school year.

Lisa and Steve made an appointment with their daughter's second-grade teacher before school began. Their child, Tonya, had done surprisingly poorly on standardized tests in first grade, and Tonya's inability to keep up with her classmates caused her self-esteem to plummet. By the end of first grade, Tonya refused to read at all. Unfortunately, her first-grade teacher was not supportive. Frustrated, Lisa worked with Tonya on her own during summer vacation, and it did help. But Lisa and Steve wanted Tonya's new teacher to know what had happened, since all the teacher had to go on otherwise was Tonya's test results.

Lisa and Steve were able to prepare the teacher about Tonya's poor self-esteem and even make recommendations as to what would make her respond positively. The teacher was wonderfully supportive and immediately began working with Tonya in ways that helped the little girl feel good about her accomplishments. By only the third day of school, Lisa and Steve got a phone call from the teacher: She had seen signs indicating that Tonya had a slight reading problem that could be corrected over time. Lisa, Steve, and Tonya's teacher worked together all year. By third grade, with extra help, Tonya was reading on grade level and her self-confidence was strong.

By the way, Lisa and Steve were both employed full-time, but they were able to develop a system with their daughter's teacher whereby they exchanged frequent notes. While there were times that Lisa — who had more job flexibility than Steve — had to leave her office for brief meetings with school staff, advocating for her daughter did not mean that Lisa had to be a stay-at-home mom.

We recommend that you not limit your school meetings to the classroom teacher. There are also art, music, and gym teachers; librarians; special education teachers. Help all of them get to know your child better.

2. **Meet with support staff, like the principal.** Far from being the scary person who hands out detentions, your school principal is the person who will help you to better understand school policies and philosophies. Your meeting with him or her will show that you're in support of your child's education and interested in working collaboratively with the district as a whole to ensure your child's success.

3. *Keep track of the curriculum and assignments.* Most districts host an annual open house at the beginning of the school year. During that time your child's teachers usually present an overview of the year's curriculum. In the lower grades you'll visit the classroom and see the more outstanding work displayed on the walls.

These experiences give you a chance to ascertain where the school wants your child to go academically and how to get the child there. Don't be afraid to ask questions as you look at the work or listen to the overview. In fact, a good question to ask your child's teacher is this: How can I best help my child academically this year? The teacher may then give you advice about how much you should help your child with his homework, for instance. With children just starting out, you may help your child best by sitting with him while he does his work and remind him of when things are due. By intermediate school your teacher might recommend encouraging your child's independence by letting him remember his assignments on his own, without frequent reminders from you.

One caveat: Do your best to attend open houses at your child's school. If you miss the meeting, you're sending your child's teacher the message, perhaps unintentional, that she or he can't count on you for support this year. If you can't make a meeting, send a note asking if you can have a short meeting at another time, or at least make a phone call.

4. *Be aware of your school support team.* Do you know who is on your local school board or who your superintendent is? Your school board, or board of trustees, is the local entity that presides over your school district. The members of that elected body have the power to make policy decisions. The school board is served by a super-intendent who makes the recommendations to the members about special programs, the implementation of aspects of the curriculum and hiring.

Every year the residents of your school district vote on the proposed school budget. Often candidates run for seats on the school board. You can make your educational preferences known in the voting booth. And you can also attend board meetings, as most are open to the public.

5. *Network with other parents.* Nothing helps more when it comes to "reality check" than having discussions with parents whose kids are the same age as yours. They can be a valuable resource and serve as sounding boards for the issues and concerns you're having.

> *When Timmy began school, Kitty quickly formed an alliance with the mother of an older child. That parent helped her navigate through the school system. She shared her experiences and worked with Kitty on issues that ran the gamut from learning how to set up a schoolbook fair to understanding how standardized tests work.*

A wonderful resource within your school district is the Parent-Teacher Association, a group of parents who work together to support teachers and school staff through parent programming and also to enhance their children's education with additional programming.

6. *Volunteer to help out.* Spending time in your child's classroom shows him how much you care about how he spends his day. Beyond underscoring your intention of collaborating with his teacher, going on a field trip or working at a class fair lets you observe how your child's teacher interacts with the children and how they interact with each other. When Jimmy comes home talking about Moose the class pet iguana, you'll then be able to participate in the conversation, having met the reptile yourself.

But it is a fact of life that such participation may be next to impossible if your work doesn't allow it. Maybe you're willing to take the occasional sick day? If not, you can still participate in ways that give your child "bragging rights" because you go the extra mile to contribute to the success of the school's programs. You can be the mom or dad who sends in cupcakes for a class party or who volunteers to cut out hearts for Valentine's Day so your child can bring them in the next day and show them off.

Nowadays, however, schools recognize that most parents work and often plan special events with that thought in mind. If you're determined to participate, you'll find the time to be at school, at your lunch hour perhaps, or in the evenings or on a weekend. A bingo night or a holiday boutique held in the evening is a perfect opportunity to attend your child's school to connect with staff in cooperative ways.

7. *Address school problems concerning your child with your partner.* When your child is having education problems, we can't stress enough that gaining knowledge about how the school functions is a task for both parents. Try to meet with your child's teacher(s) together.

The best way to motivate your child academically is for you and your partner to work together to support your children in school and be actively involved. Whether you are married, separated, divorced, or never married, your child needs to know that you share concern and investment in her education.

Being consistent in setting educational goals for your child means identifying your expectations and setting short-term goals. If your child needs help with reading, commit to reading to her every night for at least half an hour. Identify key words that are difficult and reassess them on a weekly basis. Develop a chart or system of reward to motivate and inspire your child. If math is the problem, commit to using math flash cards or, in higher grades, doing word problems or calculations together. Whatever the area of difficulty is, commit to working together in some way. If necessary, you may need to include a tutor as part of your educational team effort.

8. *Serve as a role model for lifelong learning.* Even if your experience in school was a negative one, or if you think that learning new skills is "kid stuff," you can show your child that everyone needs to practice skills, ask for help, or study to improve. Let your child see you use the dictionary to look up a word you don't know. Try new and challenging activities, like following a complicated recipe or taking up a sport you've never tried. Display an interest in new subjects and work with your child to learn more. That's what Tony and his father did one summer vacation. They spent most of their time trying to improve the family backyard deck. Tony saw his father struggle with a problem and utilize manuals and experts' input. Together they ended up building a storage shed, too.

9. *Be consistent in setting educational goals for your child.* You and your partner have to agree, for instance, that schoolwork is a priority over sports participation. Commit to the goals you set and, of course, follow through.

10. *Make sure your child is on time for school.* Believe it or not, some parents' casual attitudes toward tardiness and readiness are among the top complaints teachers have. Kids arrive at school late, half asleep, unfed, and ill-prepared for their day. Their lateness and lack of preparation can disrupt others and leave them disoriented for the day. Allowing children to be chronically late and ill-prepared sends the message that their day is not important. We want kids to know that while school can be fun, it's important and serious and something we prepare ourselves for.

11. *Schedule time for homework and studying.* Make a contract with your child. This involves clear contingencies and rewards. For example, "If you finish your homework, you can watch TV." Have

your child help to identify appropriate rewards and consequences. Have him sign an agreement. The reward should not be too excessive or too far in the future. "If you get all A's at the end of the year, then you can get a new bike" may be a great long-term goal, but there must be short-term goals to motivate and inspire him along the way. For example, "If at the end of the week your papers are nineties or above, then you earn ten dollars toward a new bike." The goal is to have the reward become intrinsic, so that your child feels good about accomplishing and achieving, but there's nothing wrong with a little external motivation. The important thing is that you're setting the tone that his work and how he accomplishes it are important. Also, monitor his homework per his teacher's recommendations.

12. **Present a united front to your child's teacher.** Don't approach your child's teacher as an opponent, even if you're unhappy about what your child has told you. Always start a teacher's meeting acknowledging the positives and thanking the teacher for her or his efforts. Be prepared with a clear statement of your concerns and a recommendation or request of how the teacher can support you and work as a team. Ask for the same, and request suggestions and guidance for addressing the problem. Commit to an approach, and arrange a time for follow-up to assess progress and improvement.

In all of these recommendations, you and your partner need to work together. When you collaborate, you set the tone in your family that your child's education matters and that you expect him to strive to be the best student possible given his capabilities and talents.

What were your school experiences as a child? What did you like most and least? Where did you excel or struggle? How did your parents view education, and what did they do when you achieved or failed? By this stage of the book it won't surprise you to learn that your answers to these questions will affect what you teach your children about the value of education. Take some time to discuss these memories with your partner to see what motivates you. How similar were your experiences?

If they differ greatly, you'll need to work together to come to common ground.

School Is Not for Moms Only

Keep in mind, too, that participation in school is not for moms only. In 1997 the National Center for Education Statistics (NCES) published a report assessing the role fathers have in their children's educational lives. The study, entitled "Fathers' Involvement in Their Children's Schools," looked at how fathers' involvement affects their child's school outcomes, such as class standing, whether they enjoy school, participate in extracurricular activities, have repeated a grade, or have been expelled or suspended.

The study found that fathers' involvement did have a distinct and independent influence on many of these outcomes. It further found that when both parents were involved in their child's schooling, there was a greater likelihood that their children in grades one through twelve would get mostly A's and enjoy school. It also reduced the likelihood that the children would need to repeat a grade. The study found that children fared worse when neither parent was involved in their schooling.

Divorced and separated dads should take note that the NCES study also found that nonresident fathers are much less likely than fathers in two-parent households to be involved with their children's school, even though it was found to be important to their children.

Combine the study results above with the fact that in our culture most moms work and many of them are employed at jobs that pay substantially lower than their spouses' jobs do. In families that cling to the stereotypes that only mothers can be involved in school, resentment can build as Mom works the same number of hours, makes less money, and then shoulders the lion's share of responsibility for her children's education.

Maybe you're wondering how you can possibly find the time. If you and your partner share the responsibility and take turns visiting the school, overseeing homework, and talking with teachers, you can do it. You and your partner are teaming up with your child's school. The power and educational achievement of this team are far greater than any single effort can realize.

And when you're a single parent, you can openly request more input from your child's school. Teachers can be made aware that you need support and ongoing communication to keep up with your children's academic performance. The school guidance counselor can act as a role model and authority figure in monitoring your child's schoolwork. Weekly sessions and contact with teachers make a difference in a child's focus and motivation.

If you're single by choice, separation, divorce, or the death of your partner, it can be even more imperative that you reach out to your school staff. You can still find ways to participate in school activities and contribute to the school environment—and receive much support in return.

Jack never thought he would have to handle parenting alone, but when his wife died of breast cancer, he became overwhelmed by the responsibilities of raising daughters who were still in grade school. Although he had often looked over homework, he hadn't been involved to the extent his wife had been. Now his eldest daughter's grades were dropping, and he didn't know what to do. Then the school social worker approached him about grief counseling for his daughters. According to his eldest daughter's teacher, she was preoccupied and withdrawn in class. The social worker helped Jack to understand that under the circumstances the girl's emotional health was more important than her academic performance. She worked with Jack, too, and two years later, when his younger daughter began expressing difficulties with a teacher, Jack reenlisted the social worker in the new family/school issue.

All parents need to reach out to their child's school staff, regardless of marital and work status. Your child's future in large part depends on it.

Reach Out at Work

Incorporating work into your village involves letting your child understand what you do and how it benefits your family. Taking your child to your job is a great way to expose and share your work ethic and commitment. If your child resents the time you spend away from home due to work, this is a great way to create understanding. Also, it gives you the opportunity to make a sensitive connection between work, responsibility, and caring for one's family.

When I was a child, my (Darlene's) parents shared their work ethic. They sometimes took me to their places of employment. Watching them interact with co-workers gave me another perspective of them as people and helped me to understand their "other world." Discussions about family finances and budgeting helped make the connection between my parents' schedule and the privileges they provided. It gave me a sense of security and self-worth to recognize that they found a way to be at every significant school and community event my brother and I participated in, despite their jobs.

Remember, as you teach children about work, more than they want any material possession, they need and actually deep down want our time and attention.

To that end, all working parents have a responsibility to keep family needs at the forefront of their employer's attention. Fortunately, many companies now offer family-friendly options like flextime, job sharing, sick care for children, and extended maternity leaves for both Mom and Dad. But these companies are still the exception rather than the norm. We firmly believe that employers need to make sure that these positive developments continue and that better options come along as well.

But you needn't wait until your boss comes to you with these options. You have an obligation to be assertive in your workplace about your needs for your family. The best time to do this is, of course, during your job-interview process. But when you have a new child, meet with your supervisor and talk about what you need in order to continue to be a productive employee. Tell your boss you're committed to your career but that you also need this support. Feel free to bring this book along as a resource in validating your position.

Research shows that productive employees who happen to be parents are also employees who perceive their supervisors as being supportive of their needs. But this perception can come only when a company puts family-friendly policies into practice. Don't wait until that happens. For your child's sake, ask for what you need.

Living the Fourth Principle

Your parents didn't need to think about the team beyond their doorstep. It was probably already in place for them. But for you, in the act of reaching out to include your extended family, friends, community, religious leaders, school and workplace in your efforts to raise your child, you're making a conscious decision. Your goals and how you go about fulfilling them will serve as valuable lessons to your child.

Be grateful that you can include the team beyond your doorstep in the daily struggles that are part of parenting. Remember that parenting is the most important job you'll ever do. There's no reason you need to do it alone.

5

Direct Your Child's Behavior: The Fifth Principle

I will be clear, firm, and consistent about my expectations as I direct my children's behavior. Along the way, my children will feel they have a voice and can make a choice.

It's true that disciplining children isn't always fun or easy. Who enjoys watching a toddler's eyes brim with tears or a teenager storm off because of something we've said or done? But if parents fail to deal with behavior issues, they fail their children. Why? Because parents accept responsibility to:

- Teach their children right from wrong.
- Mold them into productive adults.
- See that they feel happy, confident, capable, and lovable.
- Teach them to be respectful of themselves and of others.

* Model how to make responsible decisions that will help them continue to grow emotionally, psychologically, and spiritually once they've left the safety of home.

Most people think negatively of the concept of discipline, because the very word conjures up memories and images of a firm, harsh approach to controlling children. Positive discipline, by contrast, is not just a tool used for punishment and control.

The Goals of Positive Discipline

When your children misbehave, they're not out to get you (though it may sometimes feel that way). They're expressing confusion about what's expected of them and how to function in the world. They may also be expressing an emotional state, like sadness or anxiety, or seeking your attention. With that concern in mind, what are the goals of discipline? Consider these:

1. *The main goal of positive discipline is to teach children limits and boundaries.* When a preschool child acts out and hits or bites, she needs to understand that you recognize she's angry but that there are acceptable and unacceptable ways of expressing it.

2. *Another goal of positive discipline is to make sure your children learn the skills and the values that will prepare them to be independent.* You want your child to be able to make good decisions. When you discipline a child, you want him to be able to internalize the rules so that he can apply them later by himself.

3. *Positive discipline teaches children to express feelings in acceptable ways.* When you foster correct behaviors through discussion, demonstration, and guidance, you not only eliminate unacceptable behavior, you enable self-esteem and confidence to thrive. Isn't that what we want for our children?

Are You a Good Model of the Behavior You Want for Your Child?

Positive discipline doesn't usually come naturally, but every parent can learn. How easy or difficult it will be for you and your parenting partner can be assessed as you respond to the following exercise.

Think for a moment about the amount of positive discipline you exercise already in your own life. The following statements will give you a clue. Answer *Often, Sometimes,* or *Seldom.*

- I have control over my life and manage my time wisely.
- I am accountable for my mistakes and accept responsibility when I err.
- I can delay gratification.
- I express my feelings assertively rather than aggressively.
- I resolve conflicts in a mature manner.
- I show respect for others and for myself.
- I take care of my health and household.
- I know how to avoid or shed habits that impede my healthy growth.
- I select friends and activities that bolster my spirits.
- I have internalized and am willing to improve the way I work cooperatively with my partner to make the best decisions for our child.

Eleven Easy Rules for More Positive Discipline

The how to's of positive discipline start with parents learning new rules for directing their children's behavior. The following rules for parents are remarkably effective and easy to learn:

1. *You model assertive behavior for your child.*

    Example: Your son wants to go with your husband to a Yankees baseball game, and he keeps hinting around about it and then gets angry when your husband doesn't respond. You talk the problem through with him and even role-play a more assertive approach: "Dad, I really would like to go to a Yankees game. I know you have a busy schedule at work right now, but I would like it if you would take me." Privately, you might take the further initiative to alert your partner so that he's better prepared to respond appropriately to his son's request.

2. *You demonstrate positive reinforcement.*

    Example: Your daughter usually has to be told to clean her room and start her homework after school. You catch her doing it without your prompting. You praise her by saying, "You did a very good job cleaning your room and finishing your homework."

3. *You demonstrate positive correction.*

    Example: You rephrase an instruction to a positive, by telling your child what to do instead of what not to do. "Please sit nicely in your chair," for instance, instead of "Stop fidgeting in the chair."

4. *You demonstrate active ignoring.*

    Example: You ignore inappropriate behavior while praising an aspect of the behavior that was positive. A child has not finished the chore of cleaning the family room. "Thank you for helping your sister put away the toys. Now please put away the other things and vacuum."

5. *You demonstrate passive ignoring.*

Example: You ignore minor issues that appear to be attention-seeking. Your child is tapping his pencil on the table to be annoying while doing his homework. You walk away, not only giving yourself a chance to cool off but also taking away the attention to inappropriate or irritating behavior.

6. *You set up contingencies.*

Example: You make doing a desirable behavior contingent upon completing a less desirable behavior. "When you finish your book report, then you may go to the movies with your friends."

7. *You engage in adult/child consultations.*

Example: You sit down and have open discussions about problems. "Let's sit down and talk about how you're feeling. I understand that you're frustrated with your soccer coach, but do you really want to quit? We have a rule in the family that once you commit to something, you have to complete the season. Maybe we can talk to your coach about your feelings."

8. *You help your child learn a better way of doing things.*

Example: "When you slam your books on the table, I know you're frustrated about something that happened in school. Try talking to me about what you are feeling instead of just showing me that something is wrong by your behavior."

9. *You use a clear and compassionate tone with your children.*

Example: Be firm, consistent, and concise in communication. "Clyde, I asked you not to track mud in the hall. Now, please take off your sneakers immediately" instead of "How many times do I have to tell you to take off your sneakers at the front door? You never listen to me. What do you think I am, the maid?"

10. *You follow through with agreements and commitments.*

Example: If you establish a rule or promise to do something, you're reliable, dependable, and consistent. "Pat, we agreed that if you asked for candy in the store, you would not have a treat when we get home." "Joe, we agreed that if you fed the dog after school without my asking, you could watch one hour of TV."

11. *You make your expectations clear.*

Given that some things are beyond a child's control, are your expectations of her behavior understandable to your child?

Questions to ask yourself include:

- *Have I been specific enough with my child?* For example, a vague request would be "Stop leaving a mess in the family room." A more specific request would be "I would like for you to throw away your candy wrappers or your dirty paper plate each time you finish eating your snack."

- *Did I make sure my child understood what I expected?* Did I have her repeat what I expected, or did I wait for her to mess up so that I could yell and complain?

- *Did I show my child what to do?* For example, in the beginning of the process of establishing a chore such as keeping his room clean, demonstrate to your child how and when to clean up, where to put toys and clothes, and so on.

What to Expect at Every Age

But what if your child is still not responding to discipline? What other behavior are you seeing? If you see a persistent pattern or a sudden change in your child, it could be a sign that he or she needs professional help. For example:

- Refusal to comply with your positive directives.
- Withdrawal from people and situations.
- Difficulty sleeping.

- Difficulty getting along with others.

- Crying frequently and without provocation.

- Anger expressed in extreme ways.

- Frequent clinging.

- Difficulty concentrating.

These are all signs of an emotional need, particularly if they represent abrupt changes in your child. When you see this type of behavior, it's crucial to encourage expression of feelings. You can use books, toys, television programs, and anecdotes about other people to encourage discussion. Your child requires reassurance, support, and understanding as well as limits and guidance.

But all children may experience any one or more of these reactions at some point. Sometimes we're too tired or too distracted to notice, or we underestimate the seriousness of their reactions. Sometimes, though, their behavior is simply a matter of what is developmentally appropriate for them at a given age. It's important to understand what is reasonable to expect from your child developmentally. You can network with parents who have kids the same age and you can check with your family doctor and your child's teachers to get a sense of what most children go through during each stage in their development. The general guidelines below will also help you.

When it comes to determining your child's stage of development, her age is the major factor but not the only one. Your must take into account her temperament, as well as what your immediate family teaches in terms of values and acceptable behavior. How well she exhibits behaviors such as cooperation, sharing, responsibility, and compassion depends more on your teaching, modeling, and overall guidance than on anything else. Given her level and rate of maturity at any chronological age, she may struggle or have difficulty learning the various behaviors that you define as acceptable.

What to Expect from Your Toddler

Toddlers tend to have the following predictable characteristics:

- They learn that they can't necessarily have what they can touch or what they want.
- They learn the idea of sharing. It can be introduced with the understanding that it will need to be encouraged, shaped, and rewarded through praise or positive attention.
- Temper tantrums are normal, as is the word "no."
- A low tolerance for frustration is normal; so much is frustrating. There are things they want but can't reach. Items they want to open but can't figure out how. Places they want to climb but can't.

They don't yet have the language skills to express how all this makes them feel. It's no wonder there are times when they scream with rage. But you can teach them self-control by modeling how to handle frustration. In other words, no matter how much they kick and scream, try to remain calm, reassuring, and directive rather than losing control yourself.

What to Expect from Your School-Age Child

School-age children usually exhibit the following behaviors:

- They can understand empathy or being considerate of others.
- Their language skills soar, and their minds begin to be stretched with all manner of academics.
- They're becoming very social creatures as they begin to focus on their peers.
- They will emulate their peers' behaviors and language—and that can be a problem at home.
- Some back talk is normal and needs to be directed.

This is the age at which your child will say something uncharacteristic to you that, upon discussion, you learn he picked up from a friend. Don't be surprised by back talk, or even tests of your authority. But unlike with the toddler tantrum, you don't want to ignore what you consider unacceptable language or behavior. You need to state what language is acceptable in your home—and be firm about what isn't.

What to Expect from Your Adolescent

We know that as children begin to approach adolescence, they typically struggle with trying to develop their own sense of self. Adolescence is the time when:

- The issue of responsibility seems to be visited often.
- They feel the pressure and desire to be more like adults and receive accompanying privileges.
- They still struggle with childlike dependency.
- Arguments and some out-and-out rebellion against your rules are normal and need to be managed.

Teenagers often rebel as a way to individualize themselves and be separate from parents. This is the stage at which they become convinced that their parents know very little. (When adolescents reach adulthood, they'll suddenly think you got smarter, when in reality they've finally matured.) We have to take that into account when we enter into discussions with them about limits and boundaries. A child may need some space to express who she is. While she'll learn at the same time that there are some standards and guidelines you'll follow through on, she needs to be given the opportunity at least to say how she feels.

Are You and Your Partner on the Same Discipline Team?

Before you can hope to discipline your child successfully, you and your partner must form a united front. The following guidelines will make the challenge of discipline less painful for you and less confusing for your child. This is especially true for parents who are separated or divorced or for families in which one parent is frequently absent due to work. Children need consistency, or they won't know what rules to follow.

Children look to you for cues as to how to behave. Does your child's behavior serve as an unwelcome mirror, reflecting objectionable tones of voice, attitudes, or habits that remind you too much of yourself?

1. *Do you speak to each other respectfully and with love?* Do you resolve your differences calmly and with an air of mutual consideration for opposing opinions? Or do you shout at one another, perhaps even swearing or name-calling or going to the extreme of pushing or hitting? June and Ted's story may cause you to reconsider how you talk to your partner.

> *Ted worked as a corrections officer in a tense environment. When his work was done, he wanted to relax. As the manager of a greeting card store, June often worked on weekends, did paperwork at home, and made and received calls from employees. She expected Ted to help her enforce the household routine, especially making sure that the children did their chores and homework. Ted pointed out that he had his own brand of pressure in dealing with inmates all day. Yet June felt that her husband relied too much on her to organize the household.*
>
> *One of the first things Ted told us was that June spoke more warmly to her friends and colleagues at work than she did to him in front of their children. June complained about how stressful her job was and how she resented that she had to work longer hours than Ted did. Neither had proposed a discussion on sharing responsibilities at home. Instead they criticized each other and argued in front of the children. The couple ver-*

bally abused each other, and these shouting matches had esca-
lated to shoving.

Then one morning they overheard their nine-year-old son
telling his seven-year-old brother, "It's your fault Mommy and
Daddy are getting a divorce, because you're so stupid you can't
do your homework and you leave a mess all over the place."
That's when June and Ted decided to seek counseling.

Learning to work through disagreements in a healthy, life-affirming manner is key to providing your child with an illustration of good communication. In Chapter 2 we encouraged you to make peace with your partner. In Chapter 3 we spoke about communicating with compassion. Both chapters should give you the tools you need to resolve disputes with your partner. If June and Ted had followed those principles, their relationship would not have gotten to the point at which their children were disturbed.

2. ***Do you take each other for granted?*** You may be showing your children that when you live with someone for a long time, you can take him for granted. Do politeness and consideration—the manners you're sure to use with strangers—sometimes disappear once your spouse gets home? If you have a "public" face and another for home, the message you impart to your children is that they need to be on their best behavior only when others are watching. Further, family members don't warrant the same treatment we give strangers.

3. ***Do you demonstrate that you have control over your own life?*** Do you want your children to emulate the control you have over your own life? Our children look to us to learn how to manage not only their own behavior and emotions but their health, households, finances, and time. If you spend every morning searching for your car keys because you haven't established a single place to keep them, don't be surprised when your child loses his lunch box every week.

It would be illogical to expect a toddler who sees her parent melt down in a traffic jam to respond calmly when things don't go her way.

4. *Do you demonstrate the discipline of self-care?* If you and your partner take good care of your health by getting enough sleep, eating well, exercising, and practicing good hygiene, your children will learn that those habits are part of life. Just see what happens if your children see you go to bed without brushing your teeth.

5. *Is there drug, alcohol, or food abuse in your home?* Children who are exposed to drug abuse, for example, are more likely to become chemically dependent themselves.

Just as your children eventually emulate the good behaviors they see you model, they will also copy your negative side.

Partners can gently and in a nonjudgmental way support each other and try to correct undesirable habits. However, remember that you can't change anyone else. You can only support them in changing themselves. Be sure that in helping your partner, you don't become militant about changing him or her, or you'll make your partner feel inferior for his or her shortcomings. And be sure to offer praise when your partner experiences success.

How parents treat and interact with each other sets the stage for the parent/child relationship and gives your child an example to remember when he meets a new or difficult situation.

What's Your Personal Discipline Style?

From generation to generation, with each one thinking that it has hit upon *the* right way to handle misbehavior by the junior population, parents have adopted various styles of discipline. Three styles, though not equal in their effectiveness and popularity, have persisted in every generation. These are authoritarian, permissive, and authoritative.

1. *Authoritarian parents are controlling and usually do believe the "Spare the rod" maxim.* Authoritarian parents focus on limits and structure, chores, and manners. They are rigid, dictatorial, oppressive, and harsh, and they tend to dominate and humiliate. The child of an authoritarian parent may harbor feelings of anger, become overly dependent, be unable to make his own decisions, and become aggressive and hostile. Some parents who use this discipline style also use corporal punishment, which includes hitting, slapping, and pushing children.

2. *Permissive parents provide their children with little structure, believing instead that children should be encouraged to think for themselves.* Permissive parents offer their children a great deal of freedom and little or no leadership. Over time the end result for the child can be chaos and confusion. For these parents, nurturing a child has come to be synonymous with providing a never-ending supply of unconditional love, the goal being to bolster the child's self-esteem. Meanwhile, discipline has come to be thought of as cold and harsh, with control and obedience as the only goals.

3. *Authoritative parents provide their children with consistent discipline based on each child's individual capabilities.* Authoritative parents lay out their expectations and discuss their rules. Compromise is always possible. Authoritative parents don't expect blind obedience, and they use reason to discipline. These parents understand that to nurture a child is to provide consistent discipline, and they consider providing discipline an act of love. They are less concerned about being a child's friend—that is, about losing her love—than about educating, training, and rearing her. They accept that you will not necessarily lose your child's love if you're a disciplinarian. To the contrary: The desire to be your child's friend impedes her ability to accept limits.

Josh's children saw him as lenient and-fun loving. When his wife, Laura, would leave to go shopping, she would come back to a house she described as a complete disaster zone. Her frustration and anger would erupt into an argument with Josh. She would criticize him for being too lax and shirking his responsibilities as a parent by allowing the kids to destroy the house. Josh would retort that at least he knew how to have fun with the kids.

Neither Josh nor Laura felt that they were working together. Laura was always picking up after their children. After a period of struggle, the couple agreed that they had to combine their approaches to make sure their children had fun but also took responsibility for cleanup. The children actually discovered that confining their play zone to one room at a time and cleaning up as they left resulted in less cleanup time in the end. And Laura agreed to join in play more often, showing the children how she used to set up camp with blankets as tents when she was little. Josh and Laura together were able to show their children that having order doesn't preclude having fun.

We believe that children feel more secure with authoritative parenting. They know that you are there to guide and protect them and give them what they need—even though it may not always be what they want.

Up to this point, what has been your personal discipline style? Do you need to grow in your style in order to be more authoritative?

What's Your Team Discipline Style?

Before you can begin to grow in your discipline style as a team and structure a consistent set of rules for your child, you need first to analyze the way you do or don't work together now so that you can negotiate ways to share your views in the future.

1. Do you and your partner discuss methods of managing your child's behavior, or do you each follow your own plan?

Parenting as a team is all about communication first, then collaboration. Together you can brainstorm and, in cases where you disagree on strategies, come up with a compromise. We can't overemphasize how vital it is for your child to know that you care enough about him to expend the effort in discussing his behavior. Not only will his awareness of your discussions help him to internalize that his parents as a team want to work in his best interests, but your discussion (provided it's positive) also provides a model for your child about how to communicate effectively.

Additionally, when you discuss strategies together, you eliminate the possibility that your child will work to "split" you. He won't be able to play one against the other, as children so often try to do. Children can perceive differences in strictness or adherence to structure that exists between parents as an opportunity to undermine or thwart a decision of the disciplining partner. This is done when a child requests that the lenient or absent parent reverse or at least challenge what is viewed as the unfairness or unnecessary harshness of the other parent. For example, you tell your fourteen-year-old daughter that she may not go to the movies with her friends. She attempts to manipulate the situation by going to your spouse and saying, "I don't know why Daddy gets so bent out of shape when you come home late from the mall with a lot of packages. I know how you feel. I just finished all my homework, and he's being so unreasonable about letting me go to the movies with my friends. That's not fair, is it?"

As executives or heads of the family, try following these guidelines:

- Identify the discipline goal you want to achieve with your child.
- Caucus and negotiate the process by which you will establish it.
- Follow through with clear and consistent rules.

* When a transgression has occurred, support each other in carrying out the disciplinary consequences.

When we follow these guidelines, we reduce chances of splitting and unify our disciplinary approach as a strong parental team.

2. *Have you and your partner discussed how you were disciplined as children?*

You can't see where you're going if you and your partner don't know where you've been. Part of the basis for developing effective discipline strategies includes looking back on methods your parents used with you and deciding what worked and what didn't. This needs to be looked at both individually and as a couple. Take a look back at Chapter 1 and discuss it now if you haven't already done so. Together you need to review the methods used by both sets of parents and ways in which you'll incorporate or avoid them.

Insight into how your partner was raised is invaluable as you observe his or her choices of disciplinary methods. Your understanding of why your partner acts or reacts a certain way in instances where childhood memories are triggered can help you work most effectively together—just what you want your child to see. Lacking that foreknowledge, you could find yourself as mystified as your child is when her daddy overreacts in a situation that may remind him of a negative childhood experience.

You can help each other to remember that your parents' unhealthy responses to your behavior don't need to be replicated by you. Depending on your child's age, you can also explain how your own parents reacted and why you will or won't respond in the same fashion.

3. *Do you set limits and boundaries for your children?*

Do you consistently try to provide a framework for your child's daily life? Children crave and need the order and instruction you have to offer them. They look to you for guidance. If you fail to set limits and boundaries, your child will make you and himself miserable as he tries to discern for himself what's acceptable in society.

Worse still, if he's given no guidance, he may come to believe that there are no guidelines to positive behavior that apply to him. Then he'll make other people miserable, too, as he acts as though the rules for the rest of society don't apply to him.

4. *Do you trust your partner's ability to set limits and boundaries?*

As partners in parenting, through open and honest communication, you and your partner can begin to develop an understanding of each other's motivations and backgrounds. With that understanding in place, you can begin to cooperate with each other and perform as a unit. The following example illustrates what happens when a partner doesn't trust his spouse to employ discipline:

When Hugh and Candace took their son to visit friends, four-year-old Alex wouldn't always listen to instructions and suggestions. Hugh wanted Candace to be firmer in her discipline.

Once Alex was running up and down the stairs, and Candace didn't intervene. Hugh asked her to get Alex, but when she approached him, Alex ran from her, and she had to chase him. When she finally caught him, he started to hit her and yell, "Leave me alone!" Hugh was disgusted with Candace's ineffectual attempts to discipline their son. He immediately went over to Alex, swatted him on the behind, and sent him to a chair for time-out.

Power and control issues in their marriage became apparent when they came to us for counseling, and disciplining Alex was just one part of this. Alex knew that his father had the control and perceived that he didn't have to respect his mother's authority. Building a team approach required balancing their relationship and presenting a united front for Alex in order to set limits and boundaries. Hugh needed to support Candace as she learned to discipline and not give Alex the impression that "your mother can't handle it, but I can."

5. ***Once you have reached an agreement about how to handle a situation, are you both able to follow through?***

Hugh and Candace learned that effecting positive behavior-management includes balancing power in their relationship and presenting a united front. This focus needs to be consistent. While it allows for some difference in expression by both partners—you'll naturally be at least slightly different—the uniformity of approach must be maintained throughout a situation.

Life is often confusing to children. As your children wend their way through what for them is uncharted territory, they need you to provide continual direction. No sailor would rely on a compass that worked only part of the time. Nor would a child feel secure with parents who imposed a consequence one minute and ignored the same behavior the next.

More important, how can your child trust that you can give him what he needs if one of you doubts your partner's ability to do so? Children have an uncanny ability to intuit even the subtlest undercurrents of uncertainty in their parents. But that seemingly sophisticated "sixth sense" isn't accompanied by maturity. Your child's awareness of a lack of trust leads to insecurity.

6. ***Do you both have reasonable ideas in terms of what behavior you expect from your child?***

They say that knowledge is power. Certainly when it comes to discipline, knowing what's reasonable to expect from your child as she grows will empower parents. We believe that education is an important component in the development of a team approach. Go back to the section in this chapter that explains how much you can expect from your child at each developmental stage (pp. 108–111). This will provide you with assurances when you question whether or not a certain behavior is normal.

A child who can't live up to what we expect him to do begins to feel hopeless and may eventually give up trying to seek your approval.

7. *Do you and your partner believe in physical punishment?*

The decision of whether or not to resort to spanking or slapping your child is one you must make together. You must decide what form of physical punishment, if any, is acceptable to you as a unit. With the understanding that we believe any form of physical punishment to be unacceptable, you must be careful not to assign the role of physical disciplinarian to one parent. The old phrase "Wait till your father gets home" places an unfair burden on one parent and leads to the erosion of trust between that parent and the child. We'll speak more about physical punishment later in this chapter.

8. *Do you or your partner yell at or verbally abuse your children?*

We don't think that raising your voice to provide instruction or underscore the importance of an issue or express your displeasure is something about which parents should experience a great deal of remorse. As long as it's not excessive, a loud tone can sometimes be effective. But it loses its impact if you do it too often. Yelling can be habit-forming. If one parent does raise her voice, the other can help her to stay focused on what her ultimate goal is: to get the children to listen and follow her instruction. It's important to have your partner work with you to get you to understand the effectiveness or ineffectiveness of your technique.

Verbal abuse is never effective in the long run. It sets a negative example and demonstrates behavior you certainly wouldn't want your child to copy. As a parent, you need to make a contract with yourself and with your partner that you'll refrain from being verbally abusive with each other and with your children.

Make no mistake about it: Cursing at or insulting your child is abusive and can deeply damage his self-esteem. Rather than coming away having learned that his behavior is unacceptable and needs correcting, the child who is verbally abused begins to believe that *he* is unacceptable.

Further, even with yelling, but particularly with verbal abuse, if it's used constantly as a means of controlling your child's behavior, he may eventually simply tune you out. And while he may seem as if he's not listening to you at all, he won't ignore the negative message about him that you send. By the time a child begins to deafen to verbal abuse, the belief that he's no good has invaded his heart.

9. *Do either of you avoid disciplining your child for fear she won't like you?*

Remember the difference between being a parent and being a friend. While you want your child to see you as someone with whom she can speak openly and share interests, first and foremost you need to remember you're the parent. Parents have to enforce rules and guide behavior, helping their children understand what's expected. That's not what friends do.

If you're practicing positive discipline, we can guarantee there will be times when your children won't like it. But if you have learned to attach your criticisms to your child's behavior and not to the child herself, you'll model the concept, "I love you but not what you're doing."

As we discussed at the outset, providing discipline is an act of love. Convince yourself of that, and your child will come to see your conviction. Recoil from imposing consequences or setting limits, and your child will reflexively push further until you give her what she needs — boundaries.

10. *What do you do if your partner has imposed a consequence you feel is too harsh or if your partner hasn't imposed a consequence when you feel one is warranted?*

How you recover as a team when you've "dropped the ball" is crucial to your success. Suppose your partner reacted impulsively to your child's behavior with a disciplinary measure you think is too harsh. If this is how you've attempted to manage your child's behavior in the past, such a transgression is inevitable as you work to hone your techniques. Try these team steps in the future:

- Recognize the action and come together. But don't just criticize your partner or change the action in front of your children.
- Caucus privately to rethink your approach.
- Step back, discuss, and return to your child with an amended decision.

Your effort to amend a consequence teaches your child a number of valuable lessons, both in terms of how you as parents working together have decided to relate to him and how you want to relate to each other. Your child learns that it's okay to make a mistake and that solutions can be found cooperatively. Your child's knowledge of your love for him is bolstered as he witnesses your willingness to work together in his interest.

Eight More Winning Discipline Techniques

1. *Troubleshooting.*

Every parent wishes for the ideal list of discipline techniques, the one you can pull out in a moment of crisis to locate the exact response to choose. Unfortunately, discipline doesn't work that way, as you already know. What does work is communication between parents ahead of time. Waiting until your toddler is in the middle of a tantrum to determine how to handle it will likely lead to a spontaneous approach that could result in fanning the flames.

Try troubleshooting during a quiet moment together. Talk, talk, talk about your child. Once you've discussed your views on the variety of discipline issues, formulate a set of rules and responses—rules for your child to follow and responses for you and your partner to predetermine with an eye toward the types of conflicts that may arise. Consider this as troubleshooting.

Naturally, you and your partner can't predict everything that might happen, but your discussion and the agreement on the general style of your discipline will assist you when the unexpected occurs. Be supportive of each other and consistent in what you do. Let your child know that while there may be rules she's not too crazy about, she can depend on you to be clear, firm, loving, and consistent.

2. *Tell your child what to expect from you.*

Once you've begun to work together cooperatively and you've laid the groundwork for team-spirited parenting, it's time to step up to the plate with your child. Just as you educate yourself to better prepare for your child's changing development, so positive discipline involves educating your child. This means offering him a clear idea of what to expect in each new situation.

One method we like to employ is car talk. On the trip to a new activity or place, we prepare our children and make sure they know how we expect them to behave. If we're going to a restaurant or to visit a relative, we walk our children through what's likely to occur—how to respond when placing their order or when Aunt Sadie asks for a big kiss—and let them know what behavior is acceptable to use. We also want to make sure that our children know what the consequences will be if they don't follow the rules.

Probably the hardest time for you and your child is when you're out in public. That's when your convictions about limits are most likely to be tested. If your child is prepared and knows what to expect and then tests beyond that boundary, he will already know the consequence. In other words, you said he could choose a candy bar at the checkout counter of the supermarket, but the minute you walk into the store he starts asking for cookies and other items. Because you've told him the consequences ahead of time, he'll already know that as a result of that behavior he won't get any candy bar at all.

3. *Think carefully about consequences ahead of time.*

Maintaining the boundaries you've put in place will often be a test. After a consequence has been imposed, you have to follow through. That's why it's important to think carefully about those consequences ahead of time—you want to be able to carry them through. Don't make the consequence of your child's disobedience be something you don't have the heart to take away from her, like her birthday party. Just as in golf or tennis, the follow-through is every bit as important as the initial swing or serve. Otherwise, your child will come to believe she doesn't have to worry too much about your consequences, which will lead to discipline issues.

4. *Teach delayed gratification with a contract.*

We like teaching the lesson of delayed gratification with mini-contracts, such as "After you finish your homework, you can go outside and play basketball." The ability to delay gratification is an important component of self-discipline. You can help your child learn this valuable lesson by presenting him with clear contingencies. Be sure he knows what's expected of him before he moves on in his day to a more pleasurable activity.

5. *Monitor behavior from afar.*

As a child begins to grow and perhaps demonstrates that he can handle his own schedule responsibly, you can permit him to select what time he does his homework and chores. Give him a chance to show that he can be responsible and let him know when there's an area in which, because of his maturity, he can assume control over his own day. Then monitor from afar. Be certain he's aware that if he fails to act responsibly, the privilege of self-scheduling may be rescinded. Give him more choices as he grows, but make sure he knows he has to keep up his end of the contract.

6. *Allow your child to express feelings with respect.*

In fact, it's very important for parents of all children, regardless of age, to allow them to express their feelings. You can still be clear that you make the final decision, but by listening to your child's point of view, you show her you respect what she thinks and feels.

But when it comes to inviting your child's opinion about limits and rules, this applies only to adolescents. In outlining boundaries for them, there must be more discussion, understanding, empathy, and communication. We need to allow them to be more expressive, because they're developing their own adult values and beginning to learn to choose to live their lives independent of parental influence. It's crucial that your teenager feel that her viewpoints are important. Don't talk down to adolescents during discussions about responsible behavior. Being able to hear them out is important, even if at the end of the discussion you're clear the final decision will remain unchanged. In this context the solidarity of the parent team is essential, because your teenager is watching. She wants to see if you're just talking the talk but not walking the walk, that is, really doing what you say you'll do.

With every age group you have to strive to keep separate your feelings about unacceptable behavior and your feelings about your child. If your child behaves in a manner you don't want, always attach your disapproval to the behavior, not the child. Your daughter should know that while her *action* was bad, *she's* not bad. Make sure your child is secure about your love but aware that it's your job to show her how to behave.

7. *Praise and show approval.*

When you praise your child and show approval for what she does, that helps to shape her as much as do your demonstrations of disappointment for her inappropriate behaviors. Winning discipline is a combination of correction and praise. Be firm and consistent, but also make sure you're teaching your expectations in a positive way. Always ask yourself, "What am I trying to teach here? What am I trying to accomplish?"

8. *Stop and correct yourself.*

Even when you go back on what you initially agreed upon, you can stop and correct yourself. Tell your child you made a mistake, that you need to rethink your consequence and will get back to him. The lesson within the lesson is that your child will see you recognize your error and work to mend it. He'll see that you and your partner are cooperating with each other and that's exactly the message he needs to know.

Handling the "Problem" Child

Is there such a thing as a bad kid? When you read the newspaper headlines about a youth shooting his classmate and then himself, you might begin to think so.

But this is not necessarily a "bad" child. The fact is that bad behavior or even violence is a learned response. No child is born bad or violent. What we're witnessing in a violent child is typically the product of continuous exposure, shaping, and conditioning of aggressive behavior. When parents, guardians, other significant adults, and peers either directly or inadvertently reward this behavior it becomes more deeply ingrained as a preferred pattern or response. Also, if parents are in denial or ignore detrimental behavior because they are preoccupied or overwhelmed, such behavior grows unabated. Bad behavior becomes established or validated as normal, acceptable, or appropriate — and in some cases justified.

There are children who appear to have a genetic predisposition to aggressive behavior. This is usually exacerbated by environmental factors. If children don't learn to express feelings of anger, resentment, and sadness, they're more likely to act out these feelings. We believe that most kids who turn to drugs and alcohol do so for several reasons:

- They're vulnerable to outside influences, particularly their peers.
- They're seeking a place of belonging and acceptance.
- They may also be seeking fun, excitement, and thrills.
- They feel an inability to cope with life's challenges.
- They're self-medicating to deal with feelings of sadness, anxiety, or hopelessness.

Most difficult children and youth could benefit from consistent discipline. Handling the problem child involves the strategies and approaches in this chapter. The best approach is to establish a firm foundation when a child is young, but it's never too late to do so. Firm discipline or "tough love" might be necessary for a child or adolescent whose behavior has escalated out of control. We recommend that if you're experiencing behavior problems with your child that seem beyond you, seek professional help not only for your child but also for yourself. It could be the best gift you could give your family at this time. This is also a time during which you'll likely find the support of your team beyond your doorstep — your village — a welcome asset, as the following example shows:

> *Eleven-year-old Tosha came into a therapy session with her grandmother. Her mother was working. It was clear the girl didn't want to be there. She sat slumped in her chair and avoided eye contact,*

answering questions with one word and sometimes a grunt. She'd been referred to us because she was acting out at home and school and her grades had deteriorated. Although Tosha spoke little during the session, what she communicated nonetheless was powerful. When asked about her siblings, she indicated that she had two sisters and two brothers. Her answer puzzled her grandmother.

Later we learned that Tosha had included a brother that her father had with another woman. Tosha's parents had been divorced for some time, and she had little contact with her father. Her grandmother was her mother's major support. Though Tosha loved her grandmother, it was apparent she resented the fact that her father was no longer involved because her grandmother had encouraged her mother to "kick him out."

Tosha's mother felt a great deal of guilt and confusion and therefore allowed her daughter to do what she pleased. The grandmother's history revealed that she had experienced a lot of pain and many disappointments in relationships with men that she hadn't resolved. Tosha needed understanding and loving discipline. But the two adults in her life were preoccupied with their own issues, and the adult from whom she most wanted discipline was no longer part of her life.

When to Seek Professional Help

Part of helping each other as partners in parenting is to be on the lookout for behavior that is consistently problematic, even self-destructive. Every child goes through phases during which there are behavior problems. But when the problems become chronic or long-lasting, it's time for intervention by the parents acting as a team with the help of professional counseling.

What we consider behavior that is outside the norm is when your child:

- Is frequently oppositional or defiant.
- Sulks and withdraws from your requests.
- Is argumentative and defensive.
- Displays excessive teasing, taunting, or ridiculing of others.
- Makes self-deprecating remarks and statements of low self-esteem, such as "I never do anything right."

Parents usually react to these behaviors with further attempts to gain control. Setting limits is important. However, you should first seek to understand what the underlying causes and issues might be. For example, ask yourself, "Is my child seeking attention or affection from me? Is she feeling displaced by her sibling or overwhelmed with a change in our family?"

Guilt will not be a helpful response to whatever you determine about these questions because it could lead to overcompensation and indulgence. Rather, awareness, understanding, and insight are helpful. These approaches lead to positive change and modification of approaches. Remember, though, that if your well-intentioned, carefully considered team approaches don't work, you will need to seek more in-depth intervention for your child.

The Gender Factor

Males and females are different, of course, but what do these differences mean when it comes to discipline?

Experts have pointed out that boys and girls face different challenges or risk factors while growing up. For boys, major issues are school-related problems, including the fact that a larger percentage of boys than girls are diagnosed with attention deficit disorder, are in need of special education, and may become incarcerated. For girls, body image and physical and sexual harassment are primary gender issues. More girls than boys are sexually harassed and abused.

Discipline approaches must take into account some of the gender-specific issues that are of most concern in raising girls versus raising boys. For girls, this means paying particular attention to fostering positive acceptance of her body image and adjustment to physical changes associated with puberty. In addition, teaching assertive behavior in dealing with unwelcome aggression or sexual harassment is important.

For boys, specific focus is needed in developing ways to manage aggressive energy, especially within the school environment, and to encourage respect for girls. Parental monitoring of exposure to violence and aggression is gender-specific to boys when we consider the higher rate of boys in jail due to this behavior.

Let's face it: Sometimes we discipline differently based on the gender of our children. We know intellectually that we should not limit our daughters, particularly in terms of academics or sports. However, sometimes we act emotionally, overprotecting or limiting them. We realize that they need to feel empowered to achieve and excel in areas of interest, but we might not encourage or inspire them in the same way we do boys. In fact, the demands on our sons to achieve academically and excel in sports will likely be much greater. However, when it comes to preparing our daughters for life skills, we may emphasize daily household responsibilities and teach shopping skills and time management. Usually we don't expect the same degree of independence in life skills of our sons.

Most of us know that rigid sex-role stereotypes are antiquated. We know that our daughters will likely have careers and our sons need to know how to wash their clothes. But we may still harbor some traditional views of roles that affect our children's growth in all areas.

When we complained recently to our daughter that her strenuous daily workouts in gymnastics might be too much, she gave us the analogy of a male child's practicing a sport every day after school and contended that we would not say that was "too much." We realized that although we had clearly given her the message that she should excel academically, we had not given her the message as strongly about athletics. Eventually she made the decision to cut back on gymnastics, but she replaced it with tennis and basketball.

In Darlene's family of origin, her brother was the athlete and Darlene excelled academically. Our daughter, Dotteanna, was clear that she wanted to be different. She was able to show discipline to maintain honor-roll status while doing gymnastics training. Though it was not our interest, we had given her the foundation of discipline to manage her time doing what was her passion.

Discipline is guidance, and what we focus on and reinforce is likely what our children will excel in, regardless of their gender. We need to guide them away from negative influences and toward positive influences. Boys should not be given the message that "boys will be boys" when they misbehave or engage in troublesome behaviors. Girls should be afforded the same opportunities to make mistakes and learn from them without being made to feel shame and guilt. This is particularly true during the adolescent period and around sexuality. We should give boys the same messages and discipline as girls, particularly that they should value their bodies and make wise choices regarding their sexual experiences. Certainly we want our children to abstain, but we must prepare them for this by teaching them self-respect and respect for others.

When it comes to discipline, gender has no place in your methods and practices. Discipline your male and female children equally, so that they don't go out into the world believing a stereotype such as that one gender is more likely to have behavior problems and the other needs special treatment to succeed.

Negative Lessons of Physical Punishment

When you spank, shove, or use any other physical punishment, usually all you're accomplishing is ridding yourself of anger. But for your child it's a lesson that the way in which you resolve problems is by hurting someone. It's a lesson that when you're out of control, force is the answer.

Physical punishment is inappropriate because it sets a model of aggression in a society in which children are already exposed to too much violence. Taking a belt to your child will not teach him to be nonviolent. All too often we hear of parents who punish their son for hitting his sister by hitting the boy "to teach him a lesson." The only lesson they're teaching their child is a confusing one that says, "Do as I say, not as I do" and "Violence is okay for me, but not for you." Children will see you as contradictory and hypocritical. Eventually you'll lose their respect, and over time your disciplinary measures will fall on deaf ears.

There are times that safety issues or an emergency arises when you would restrict your child's movement to prevent her from hurting herself. Sometimes if a child has lost control, we may snatch her and put her in a seat. We don't think this is excessive. At times children do need external control.

But you invite trouble when you routinely use a physical approach to discipline. Typically what children will do is internalize their anger about it and express it other ways, as through nightmares, or displace it onto other people. You see this often with the schoolyard bully. Frequently bullies are the victims of harsh physical punishment at home and have learned to act out their frustration by abusing someone smaller.

Time-out for Parents

We strongly believe in "time-out" as a way of expressing your disappointment with your child's behavior, as well as a way to help her regain her self-control. A temporary withdrawal of attention is much more effective than the ongoing, even continuous yelling and spanking that some parents use. In fact, your kids will learn a valuable self-management lesson if they watch you give yourself a time-out. You want to make sure that the discipline process doesn't include drama or something that turns into a reward for misbehavior. You want to minimize that kind of attention and focus more on being firm and clear, without a lot of unnecessary side effects.

It's important for you to know how to remove yourself from a situation that is escalating and getting out of control, particularly with a teenager. Give yourself a time-out. Say, "I need some time to think about this" and remove yourself from the situation so that you can focus and concentrate on the best approach to handling the situation. You can even take this time-out with your partner. You may say, "We need to stop this discussion now, since it's not going in a positive direction."

You can also ask for the support of your network. Call your neighbor, your mother, or your church friend and ask if he or she can stop by while you make a quick escape to the store for milk.

> *Delia, mother of two children, was having a late-afternoon coffee break in her kitchen with her friend Lee. Then two-year-old Pamela spilled her milk, and Andrew, age three, started stamping his feet in it, sending milk splashing everywhere. Delia started yelling at the children and crying simultaneously. It was the last straw during an exhausting day for her. "I've got to get out of here," she announced, sobbing. Without waiting a moment longer, she turned to signal a time-out hand motion to Lee who grabbed the children's jackets and a diaper bag, and ushered the children to her house around the corner for an unexpected play date. The kids, who loved Lee's dog, were thrilled. An hour later Delia returned, smiling and a little chagrined. But she was now ready to face her children cheerfully.*

Don't worry if you're one of those parents who has to lock herself in the bathroom for five minutes—first making sure your child is safe—in order to blow off steam. When you give yourself time to calm down, you can unlock the door to a whole new situation, rather than one in which your anger escalates in proportion to how much your child defies you. Self-control and compassion will likely follow. When it comes to handling your child's behavior, it's the only discipline path to choose.

Living the Fifth Principle

Always remember that directing your child's behavior is an act of love. Once you realize that discipline can be a positive way to nurture your child's growth, the stage will be set for managing aspects of family life that can get out of hand.

6

Nurture the Sibling Bond: The Sixth Principle

I will love each of my children as individuals, and I will take time to let each of them know that I appreciate their unique talents. When they differ, I will be patient and accept normal conflicts while guiding them toward resolution and harmony.

Comedian Bill Cosby once joked, "Desperately you try to calm your daughter while wiping her face and seeking the name of the person who reduced her to this state. But your plans to kill this person are changed when you learn that the person is another daughter of yours."

There will never be anyone else in your life who shares your childhood experiences quite like siblings. They're your confidantes when you need to complain about Mom and Dad. They're your playmates on a rainy day. They're the ones who help you carry on family traditions and can help you gain perspective and insight about past family hurts. They're the ones who do everything first so you can learn from their mistakes and successes or the ones who follow you everywhere, seemingly in awe of you.

They're members of your generation in a way even friends can't be. Your friends may come and go, but your siblings are for keeps.

Yet there rarely has there been a sibling relationship untouched in some way by rivalry since biblical times. Remember the brothers Cain and Abel?

All the teasing, the backseat arguing in the car, and the seemingly petty jealousies about who had more candy for dessert can drive parents crazy. But expecting siblings to get along without conflict is neither realistic nor healthy. Loving families need a middle ground. Thank goodness there are significant benefits for children in their rivalry. That may even be a helpful mantra you can repeat to yourself as they bicker. In fact, the initial step you must take toward developing strategies that ensure your children's healthy rivalry is your acceptance that it's normal and that all of your children will move in and out of it. You can't have siblings without rivalry—every relationship has differences.

The Positive Side of Rivalry

In reality, sibling rivalry is not all bad. In fact, believe it or not, in some ways sibling rivalry is actually a good thing. Within the conflicts and day-to-day bickering, your children are learning valuable lessons that can eventually bring them to a place of love and friendship.

With team-spirited guidance from you and your partner, sibling rivalry can benefit your children in the following ways. It can:

- Help them learn to get along with others. There's no better practice ground for kids to learn how to relate to peers than the safety of their own home.
- Provide them with challenges that prompt them to learn to seek understanding and solutions with others.
- Teach them the art of compromise and negotiation.

- Help them develop an awareness of others and a consideration for other people's feelings.

- Instruct them that "life is not fair" and assist them in learning to cope with this fact of life.

- Help them learn patience and tolerance of differing views.

- Eventually, offer them not only the support of their parents as they move through their endeavors but also the support and encouragement of their brothers and sisters.

- Give them an opportunity to witness how their siblings handle success and failure.

- Give them insight into themselves and others.

- Allow them to discover someone else's boundaries and learn how to assert their own.

You want your children to be assertive, to express their opinions, to differ with each other, to be able to compromise with each other and negotiate through conflicts. For example, Dawn and Cassandra are both good students and are in their school's drama club. There have been times when they've tried out for the same part in the school play. Their parents encourage them both and cheer them on, but they know realistically that only one or neither one will get the part. As a family, they have developed their own traditions for supporting each other, which helps with the rivalry. They celebrate both girls' efforts and achievements in academics and theater. Tennis stars Venus and Serena Williams's parents apparently have the same philosophy.

This doesn't mean, however, that the only child is either better off or destined for a life of social problems. It simply requires that you provide more opportunities for socialization and family relationships with cousins and other relatives. Strong peer relationships also offer only children ways to enhance their social skills.

How Does Sibling Rivalry
Get Started?

Sibling rivalry originates from a young child's nearly primal, instinctual urge to be the focus of his parents' attention. In infancy and through their early years, children are developmentally egocentric. That is, they truly believe that the world revolves around them. Your purpose, as they see it, is to meet their every need—right away!

Who hasn't been surprised to hear the screams of an infant who sounds as if he's being tortured? Rushing to his aid, you see that he's frantic because he dropped his rattle, and you think to yourself, "It seemed like an emergency." Insight into how your baby's mind develops provides the answer. Time to young children means only "now." The present is all there is; they have no concept of "wait a minute." If a baby is uncomfortable because she's wet, she thinks the discomfort will last forever.

The stage is set for sibling rivalry when the baby has to wait for your attention because you're occupied with her sibling. Young children—toddlers and preschoolers—still operate with what may seem to adults as a skewed sense of time, so they, too, can't wait.

Your child's dependency on you in his earliest years is profound. For his survival, he must rely on you to meet his needs. When something takes you away from total focus on that, he becomes fearful and eventually angry. The target of his anger is often the individual, the intruder, who took you away from him—his sibling. Infants can feel the presence of that other focus as a threat to their very lives.

Working as a team, you and your partner can do a lot to calm those fears. You can provide reassurance as your babies learn to internalize the fact that you'll be there for them. But as parents of more than one child, you can't—and shouldn't—give them what they really want, which is your constant, undivided attention.

Even given how common sibling rivalry is, as a parent you may feel that only your children act this way. Take a look around at the playground, the toy store, your own siblinghood. If you're honest, you can't help but notice that most brothers and sisters fight. Talk to other parents and they'll say what you always say: "Why can't they just get along?"

It may seem to you, however, that disputes between your children are more intense than those you experienced. With more and more families choosing to have fewer children, the level of those arguments can seem heightened. Years ago, in large families of four or more children, siblings offered each other more of a buffer as their competitive feelings were spread among more children. In today's families, in which two children are more common, those children have only each other as targets for their anger at not being the only one.

Even the best efforts of parents to forge and maintain a team relationship can be derailed by sibling rivalry. You each have your own feelings about mediating fights between your kids, individual thresholds for kid-related commotion, your own concerns and fears about your children's futures, and your own preferences among your children (more on that later).

We're experienced psychologists and parents, and we're the experts writing this book, so there's no such thing as sibling rivalry in the Hopson household, right? Wrong, because the fact is that every family faces sibling rivalry issues. The difference is in how they're handled, before they become too serious.

For example, Dotteanna is thirteen, and Derek Jr. is seven. But just a year ago there were times when our son would spontaneously hug us a little tighter and a little longer at bedtime or when they both left for school. Inevitably, Dotteanna would say something bossy or negative to him, like "D.J., make sure you get your lunch box. You always forget it." Her tone would be harsh.

As alert as we try to be, it took us a little while to see the connection. Although she receives a great deal of attention, too, Dottie was envious of her brother's style of getting it. At twelve she wanted to show how much more independent and mature she was than D.J. But she resented the extra hugs and kisses he received.

We cherish that fact and didn't want to overlook that she'd still hold our hand while shopping in the mall, still cuddled with us to read a book, still liked to be tucked in at night, and still playfully grabbed for an unexpected hug. So even now, often when D.J. initiates an extra hug, if Dottie is around, we suggest a family hug. She joins in, and she no longer has that critical reaction to her brother. (It's important to remember that even as children get older, they still enjoy affection and being "babied" at times. This is especially true if a younger sibling receives a great deal of affection.)

D.J. has his own jealousy issues about his older sister. Dottie's gymnastics training requires a lot of our time and attention. Many weekends we're at meets to cheer her on. D.J. began to tumble and flip around the house to get our attention. He would also make noise and distract his sister when she was practicing on her beam at home. We tried to praise him for his interests and abilities in gymnastics, but we realized it wasn't enough, nor was it the right approach. When we enrolled him in a boys' class, he excelled. We also wanted him to have his own interests, so we videotaped him swimming and we enrolled him in basketball.

Now when we watch the tapes of Dottie's gymnastics, we can show tapes of D.J. swimming, playing basketball, and doing his own gymnastics routines. This experience reemphasized for us that children need praise and attention for their individual interests and accomplishments.

But as normal as sibling rivalry is, it does have its limitations. For example, siblings' playful teasing is a healthy way of demonstrating their affection. However, hurtful statements and intense competition are unacceptable, and this should be made clear in every family very early on. Statements such as "I hate you" should be seen as inappropriate and not to be tolerated. Teaching children how to express feelings of anger and hurt to a sibling is an important life lesson (see Chapters 3 and 5).

What other issues should you anticipate among siblings? What factors, perhaps beyond your control, influence their rivalry? Let's take a look.

The Role of Age Differences

You've probably heard all the theories about spacing when planning children, such as that the ideal spacing between siblings is three or four years, so each child has a chance to get attention from Mom and Dad. That a six-year spacing or more makes the children of different generations, so they have little in common. That a boy and girl won't argue as much as same-gender siblings, because they each have their own interests.

The fact is that no matter how many years between siblings or what their gender, no matter their differences, they share you, and that alone makes for sibling rivalry. However, we do find that siblings who are close in age often grow up to be different in terms of personality, views, and interests. They search for ways to be different and to show their individuality and to feel special. It's how they demonstrate their unique qualities and how they gain parental attention. Finding areas in which to shine that don't compete with a sibling is a way to inspire harmony and unity in the family system, while obtaining recognition.

Toddlers as Siblings

In general, the toddler will have difficulty sharing the attention of siblings. He'll be more demanding at this stage and will act out to seek attention in inappropriate ways if he feels jealous. This is particularly difficult if the child feels displaced by a newborn.

At this stage, no is the favorite response to most situations, and requests to get along with a sibling will undoubtedly result in the same, at least initially. It's a symptom of independence, despite the toddler's need to earn your love and attention. Sublimation is learned and expressed during this period, so while your child knows he can't hit his new baby sister, that won't stop him from tossing her toys around dangerously close to her head. It stands to reason, then, that you would never leave a toddler alone with a baby.

Helping your children develop a loving sibling bond is one of the best gifts you can give them. It can start as early as when an only child is told that a new sibling will be joining the family. Whether this is occurring through birth, adoption, or marriage it's important to guide and prepare your child in how to relate to the newly arriving sibling. For our family, we chose to have Dotteanna accompany us to prenatal office visits. We talked regularly about how we felt she could help out with Derek Jr. also, letting her know that we expected she would be a loving and caring big sister toward her brother.

Preschoolers as Siblings

Preschoolers begin to move from parallel play and interactions to more engagement and exchange. They're learning to cooperate and share material things and attention. They tend to want to "tattle," sometimes seeking to find fault with their sibling to be able to report "bad behavior" to a parent.

School-Age Children as Siblings

School-age children typically demonstrate sibling rivalry by aggressing or withdrawing. A child might act out and yell, "I hate him" about a sibling if she perceives him as gaining preferential treatment from a parent. She might withdraw and feel a sense of hopelessness and frustration. This is particularly true, for example, if a child feels she cannot measure up to parental expectations as well as her sibling can. Other challenges involve wanting space and possessions of one's own, particularly not wanting to share a room, clothes, or games. But siblings this age will have fun interacting and participating in games and activities together, and there's a focus on fairness and equity among them.

Adolescents as Siblings

There's a real thrust toward autonomy and a need to be seen as an individual among adolescents, as well as a need to express an independent spirit and be able to form their own judgments and attitudes. Their ideas appear to be radical and have to challenge parent's views. They're sensitive to comments and remarks from siblings and are highly egocentric, feeling that "no one understands me." They want to have their own accomplishments and interests, separate from siblings. This is a time at which adult siblings can recall having felt a self-imposed isolation from one another. There's a great need for respecting each other's privacy and solitude. This is particularly true in terms of friendships and "secrets." The issues around protecting one's space, clothing, and possessions are heightened.

How Do Your Children Actually Get Along?

Throughout this book we've asked you to evaluate your own background and that of your partner in terms of parenting issues. Now we're asking you to extend that introspection to your children. Let's start with this inventory.

1. Do your children argue frequently?
2. Do your children demonstrate envy when one attains or accomplishes something?
3. Do your children engage in mean-spirited teasing?
4. Do your children sabotage one another's efforts?
5. Do your children play and laugh together?
6. Do your children help each other with homework or housework?
7. Do your children support and defend each other with other people?
8. Do your children miss each other when apart?

9. Do your children do special things for each other, like bring home a gift from a class trip?
10. Do your children apologize to one another?

The first four questions focus on behaviors that you expect to be infrequent between your children, and the remaining questions focus on behaviors you hope your children will engage in. Have you made your expectations clear to each of your children? Do they know what you will tolerate and what you will not? Focusing on what you would like your children to experience with each other will help them to develop it.

What you hope to see are some positive reactions between siblings. Do your children ever express loving reactions to one another? Do they seem to enjoy each other, expressing affection and warmth more often than hostility? When they disagree, do they do so in a way that shows respect for each other, or does every tiff lead to character attacks? It's important for you to keep their relationship in perspective.

Kate grew up in a household she describes with a shudder as a "battleground." Her four siblings, following the lead of their parents, were verbally and physically abusive toward one another — and loud. It seemed there was never the quiet that Kate craved. She spent a lot of her childhood in her room or alone outdoors, hiding from the chaos. She vowed that when she had children, her household would be serene and loving.

But with two boisterous and energetic sons, she cringes every time they raise their voices and cuts off every disagreement. "Don't you love your brother?" she'll ask one of the boys. Shamefaced, the boys will temporarily quash their natural tendency to assert themselves, until next time.

Their father, Bill, also grew up in a loud and demonstrative household. But he was usually found right in the middle of the fray, doling out as many punches and insults as he received. He relished the excitement his rowdy siblings could generate. When Kate complained to him about the frequency of their sons' disputes, Bill would reply, "That's nothing. One time my brother broke my tooth with a plastic bat."

Clearly Kate and Bill have disparate responses to their children's rivalry. Kate can't bear any conflict, while Bill barely notices. To operate as a team, Kate and Bill need to make a realistic assessment of what's going on in their home. They need to acknowledge their vastly differing levels of tolerance for conflict and come to a middle ground of what is "normal" for their family.

Assistance could be found through a third party. By enlisting the aid of friends who have children, teachers, or even the children's grandparents, the couple could learn to gauge whether their boys' bickering falls within the parameters of normal rivalry and high spirits.

Here is a chart that can help you determine whether or not your children's interaction is normal or excessive:

How Do Your Children Interact?

Normal	Excessive
Raising voice	*Getting physical: pushes, hits, punches*
Teasing within limits: "I'm gonna kick your butt in this game. I'm the pro; you're the rookie."	*Taunting with ridicule or hostility:* "You'll never beat me. You're such a wimp. You can't score one point; you're a punk."
Distancing: "I don't want you to come in my room when my friends are here."	*Embarrassing:* "Look, shadow! My friends are here. Get lost!"

What Children Usually Fight About

Most siblings argue about fairness. To many, "That's not fair" is a mantra. For instance, the Caldwells were having an "unfairness" problem with their two sons.

> *"If I have to count out the exact same number of Cheerios one more time, I'll go nuts!" Alice exclaimed. Her husband, Ray, pronounced wearily, "These kids are going to grow up being the pettiest and most selfish people I've ever seen."*
>
> *It seemed as though at every meal or anytime there were treats to distribute, the Caldwell kids clamored for precise equality. Back and forth, Alice would find herself adjusting the level of milk in their cups. Meanwhile, Ray feared that his children's lack of desire to share would lead them to lonely adult lives with no friends, no families of their own. Alice strove to ensure that each child received everything equally, while Ray perceived their selfishness as a sign of moral decay.*

Parents working as partners eventually learn to refrain from buying into child-generated guilt trips. They learn that the healthy goal for parents of more than one child is fairness and that fair doesn't always mean equal. Children seem to have a very highly developed sense of equality. As a parent, you need to impart that fair is not always equal. If you look deeper under the cries of "It's not fair," you'll likely discover a wish for exclusive attention. Beneath that expression is your child's need to know she's heard and appreciated for her individuality.

It will be best for all concerned if you accept the futility of struggling for absolute equality. Together with your partner, stay out of the trap of scrambling to provide the exact same for every child. Avoid telling your children, "I love you all the same." That denies your children the joy of knowing that what is unique about them is cherished.

Being fair, not equal, means you give to each child according to individual need. If you have a child who seems to be forever keeping score, unspoken under that is the fear you love his sibling more. If you as parent endeavor to provide absolute equity after a fairness complaint, you can often be manipulated into rushing to prove you don't love the other child more. That scenario cannot have a good outcome.

When Children Are Most Likely to Fight

Children are more likely to fight when they feel jealousy, envy, insecurity, and a violation of privacy. In addition, they'll get riled up if they perceive a sibling as receiving preferential treatment from you or your partner. But children also argue as a reaction to tension in your home.

> At the end of another grueling day at the office, Ginger wearily mounted the steps to her child-care provider's house to pick up her three daughters, Debra, Heather, and Kathy. Today was the first day the girls had stayed with a sitter after school since Ginger had gone back to work. She was nervous because the girls had been arguing a lot lately as a result of the financial stress the family was under.
>
> "How did it go?" she asked warily.
>
> "Wonderfully," the sitter enthused. "They get along so well."
>
> Ginger was in shock as she ushered the girls to the car. The door of the sitter's house had no sooner closed when Kathy bellowed, "I get the front seat!" triggering a chorus of "No, I do!" from her sisters. Ginger looked on in horror, momentarily asking herself, "Why can't they behave for me?"
>
> Their father, Len, arrived home just as the girls bolted into the house. Seeing him, the trio exchanged their teasing and taunting for excited squeals of "Daddy's home!" Later, when Ginger

relayed her surprise at the sitter's observation, Len said, "I never have a problem with them, either." Ginger, exhausted and feeling invalidated thought, "What am I doing wrong?"

Probably nothing. A recent study performed by Marcia Summers, Ph.D., professor of educational psychology at Ball State University in Muncie, Indiana, demonstrated that children argue most in front of their mothers. We would add that this is particularly true with daughters.

But equally important is the impact that changes in your lifestyle may have on your children. Ginger's return to work calls for the realization that her absence may trigger her daughters' feelings of loss and fear. This is a time when they need extra reassurance from their mother—and a time when she needs extra support from Len. His comment that he doesn't have a problem implies that the conflicts are solely Ginger's fault. Rather than placing blame, Ginger and Len need to work together to get their family through this challenging time.

When to Seek Professional Help

Is one of your children the victim of constant assaults from his sibling? Does he seem afraid of his brother? When Ricky burst through the house after school in tears, with another bruise forming on his cheek, Lina knew that it was his big brother Todd who had hit him for no apparent reason. "We got off the bus, and I started walking, and he hit me for no reason," cried Ricky.

Deep inside, Lina knew that there was something wrong with the way Todd treated his little brother. He couldn't seem to walk past the boy without hitting, pinching, or slapping him. Ricky's very presence on earth seemed to incense Todd. Lina quelled the worry and instead became exasperated with Ricky: "Why can't you just stay away from him? You know how he is. Or even better, why don't you fight back?"

Things didn't improve for Ricky when his father, Pete, got home. Looking across the dinner table at the boy's bruises, Pete seemed disgusted at his younger son's weakness. He remembered how his older brother had hit him and how eventually he got strong enough to retaliate. As Todd walked past Ricky, he smacked his brother on the head, setting off another mealtime ruckus, with Ricky crying, Todd denying he'd done anything wrong, Lina castigating both boys, and Pete criticizing her for allowing another supper to be ruined.

The family needed help. Todd had tacit permission from his parents to act out violently toward his brother. Ricky had been abandoned by both his parents, and believe it or not, so had Todd. The children's abusive relationship took Pete back to his own unresolved family of origin issues, while Lina lacked the emotional health to listen to the inner voice that told her something was wrong.

The couple had to seek professional intervention before Ricky was seriously injured. The entire family needed to learn that while it's okay and even healthy to feel anger, it's never acceptable to act out one's anger physically.

Has nonstop fighting among your children extended to problems outside the home with friends, schoolmates, and authority figures?

May and Jeff had begun to dread parent-teacher conferences for their three children, who are less than a year apart and range from age seven down to five. This year their youngest son, Matthew, was in kindergarten, so they had three sets of teachers to meet with. They heard only slightly different versions of the same story from the trio of teachers: "Matthew slapped another child during gym." "Helene bit a classmate in the library." "Jared has just been released from suspension for punching the lunchroom monitor, who tried to break up a fight."

As they have been since the fighting started (practically when the three were still in diapers), Jeff and May were at a loss. "All kids fight, don't they?" they said.

Not like this. The brawling that had been largely ignored at home had become a way of relating for the three children. Jeff and May, while often shocked at their children's capacity for violence, had never been able to set limits or impose consequences. Now that the school was imposing the consequences, such as suspension, the couple was at an even greater loss as to how to keep their children from hurting themselves and others.

Again, this was a situation that called for professional intervention. Jeff and May needed to be brought to the realization that their ineffectual disciplining had resulted in the failure of Jared, Helene, and Matthew to learn healthy coping skills and impulse control.

When nonstop fighting, even if it's on the less extreme level of simply contrary attitudes, begins to spread out beyond your home, sibling rivalry is at its most severe.

Seven Recommendations for Reducing Rivalry

To what extent have you learned to stem rivalry's rise from flow to flood? Earlier you evaluated how your children interact with each other. The following inventory will provide you with insight into the way you interact with them.

1. Do you spend individual time with each of your children?
2. Do you communicate better with one child than with another?

3. Do you listen attentively to all of your children when they're talk-ing as a group?

4. Do you share a common interest or activity with each child?

5. Do you see one child as easier to relate to?

6. Do you and your partner defend one child more than another?

7. Do you and your partner argue a great deal and/or get physical during disagreements? In front of your children?

In an ideal situation, your answers to these questions should be yes for numbers 1, 3, and 4 and no for numbers 2, 5, 6, and 7. Let's take a moment to examine why.

Recommendation Number One: One-on-One Time

First of all, nothing goes further toward quelling sibling rivalry than your working to assure your children that you value what is special, dear, and unique about each one of them. Looking back at the case of Alice and Ray, what's beneath those requests that everyone gets the same amount of Cheerios is the children's desire that each receives an equal measure of attention.

Time apart from their siblings is good for children's independence, their autonomy, their imagination, and their growth and development. It's important to allow individual time, not only with you but also with their peers, their friends, or just alone in their room. For example, Derek takes D.J. to basketball, and Darlene has spent many hours with Dot at gym-nastics. We both watch them play individually at tennis lessons. We have also switched the activity each of us attends to create balance and variety in parental attention for each child.

There will be times, too, when your child wants to play with his sibling's friends. There needs to be compromise and negotiation around sharing friends. Sometimes children should be encouraged to play as a group, and other times privacy should be given. It's best to decide and plan ahead of time before visitors come. This allows for transition time and acceptance of the arrangement.

Recommendation Number Two: Equal Communication

It's only natural that as your children progress through stages of development, you find one child easier to talk to. Perhaps your son is at that adorable (and fleeting) stage when he seeks your approval and views you as the expert on every issue, while your daughter has entered adolescence, with its compulsion that she rebel and separate from you. Why wouldn't you feel more comfortable speaking with an eight-year-old whose eyes glow at your brilliance rather than with a thirteen-year-old who rolls her eyes at every word you say?

Feeling more comfortable with one child is okay, but expressing it isn't. We can't emphasize enough how important it is to put in the extra effort to communicate with the child who is more challenging. Not to make that effort is to send the message you like one child better. Find a hobby to do together. Identify what your child likes, and develop mutual interests. If you don't, she'll feel alienated and become vulnerable to negative peer pressure, searching for a sense of belonging.

Recommendation Number Three: Listen Attentively to All

In our practice we often hear from children or observe for ourselves that their parents focus more on what one child is saying compared with the others. It seems as if they value more what one child has to say when he or she is given more of "the floor." As a parent, you must strive to be an attentive listener to each child. Instead of cutting off or interrupting the child, you need to learn to reflect back to him what you're hearing. The technique of reflection, or restating in your own words what your child has said, demonstrates to him that you've heard him. When your children are expressing themselves in a group setting, particularly during a dispute or conflict, in reflecting back what they've expressed you let each of them know that he or she will get an equal opportunity to be heard.

Recommendation Number Four: Share a Common Interest

In addition to individual time with Mom or Dad, children need you to focus on what they're interested in. Sharing an enjoyable activity with your son makes it clear that you value him as a unique individual. If you have no common interests, your child needs to know you're willing to extend yourself to learn more about and become more involved with something he's interested in.

This is particularly crucial if you do share an interest with his sibling. For instance, Daisy is a single mother of two sons. Her nine-year-old is a video game fanatic, something Daisy has no interest in. But because it's the only topic her son will talk about with her, she listens carefully and asks questions, and recently she found some articles about his favorite game for them to read together.

One of the main ways you can demonstrate that you value your child as an individual is to focus on her talent. If you have a strong interest in basketball and your child is a great player, it's fine to share that with her. But make sure you don't develop a greater bond with her than with her nonathletic sibling. Be extra careful not to alienate the other child or have either child feel that she's getting your love and attention because she's excelling in that one particular area.

Recommendation Number Five: Relating to All

Of course, if you and your child share the same interests and she's at an easier stage developmentally, you'll find yourself more comfortable with her than with the one who isn't. Again, we remind you that while you may feel this way, it's important that your own behavior doesn't mirror your feelings.

It's ironic, but it's during a difficult stage in development when your children most need to know that you love and accept them. As you instruct your children that it's okay to have negative feelings but not okay to act them out, you must also walk that walk. From time to time you may feel that you don't want to spend a single minute with your sullen teen or bossy fourth-grader. It's then that you need to make the extra effort to find a way to relate to that child in a positive fashion. To do so, we want to reinforce tips offered earlier:

- Model acceptance and enthusiasm.
- Demonstrate positive reinforcement with praise.
- Use positive correction, as in "Please say a positive thing about your brother."
- Actively ignore.
- Passively ignore.

Recommendation Number Six: Treat Them Equally in Conflicts

Perceiving one of two children as the "weaker" benefits neither of them. The "stronger" child, the one who earns the blame for conflicts and perhaps the lion's share of punishments, begins to feel over time that she's not loved as much. Meanwhile, the "weaker" child may become manipulative, using his weakness as a way to gain power and control in your family. When disputes break out, you and your partner need to work to assess the situation calmly rather than rush to blame one particular child.

You also need to keep your expectations for your children aligned with their capabilities. Often the oldest child can become caught in the "you should know better because you're older" trap. You must be careful not to turn your oldest into a third parent. Let him have an opportunity to enjoy age-appropriate experiences and emotions. That way you can avoid the resentment that occurs because the older child has too much responsibility and the younger child feels bossed around.

Recommendation Number Seven: Fewer Arguments and No Physical Battles

Your kids don't need to be an audience to constant bickering or, worse yet, physical violence. The emotional damage this causes is beyond what you and your partner could ever imagine. The tension, anxiety, and fear potentially instilled in your children are effects that can be long-lasting, continuing well after the topic of the argument or fight has been forgotten. Children who observe parents arguing constantly will tend to emulate this behavior and view confrontation as a way to manage disagreements. They can also become fearful of addressing conflict because they are afraid any disagreement will escalate into violence.

Growing Away from Rivalry

Here is a brief overview of how you can help your kids move through stages of rivalry as they grow:

The Preschool Stage

- Keep in mind that your children aren't born with an innate ability to resolve conflicts.

- Expect your children to be responsible for their behavior, but beware. Asking too much too soon or too little too late backfires. Children feel pressured and overwhelmed when excessive responsibility is placed on them, and they don't learn responsibility when too little is placed on them. Their sense of independence and accomplishment is thwarted.

- Very young children from infancy through preschool years can't be spoken to as if they're miniature adults and be talked out of their conflicts with each other. Until you show them different, their instinct is to attempt to resolve their arguments physically.

- You have to provide consistent outside control, usually in the form of separating the children and time-outs when disputes erupt.

The Grade-School Stage

- During early grade-school years, kids start to learn that you have to give to get, and they're ready to learn the basics of negotiation and compromise. At this stage you can provide guidance and suggestions for compromise.

- Later on in grade school, as they've learned the benefits of negotiation, siblings can begin to agree on rules and make contracts with one another, such as "Don't go in my room and I won't go in yours." At this time, too, there's an intense need for things to be exactly fair. You can continue to help them resolve their conflicts by listening attentively and making suggestions. This is also a good time to encourage team competition as an outlet to channel their competitiveness.

The Adolescent Stage

- During adolescence, children learn to empathize. They can respond to the question "How would you feel if . . . ?" and can put themselves in another's place. They begin to emulate the family values that they've seen modeled. Their morals are beginning to develop, as is mutual respect for others, combined with a strong desire to be a recipient of that same respect.

- Remember that children move very slowly through their stages of development. Sometimes there's a step forward and then a retreat. You first notice this with a preschooler who regresses when a new baby comes into your family. Suddenly she wants a bottle and begins to talk baby talk. If you can allow that regression for a time and offer increased reassurance of your love, she'll return to her earlier maturity. But keep in mind that without reasonable parenting responses to sibling rivalry, adolescents can get stuck in a stage, too.

The Trap of Favoritism: Try Not to Make It Worse

How do you feel about losing and disappointment? Were you taught it doesn't matter how you play the game, that winning is the only acceptable outcome for you? Then you will probably relate strongly to this story:

Brian and Marty are both handsome boys who excel at sports. But Marty, the older, is by far the more gifted athlete and has been since he was a preschooler. As a seventh-grader he's already been selected to participate on the high school varsity basketball team. Both his father, Scott, and mother, Holly, were accomplished athletes during their school years, and they place great value on "being the best." Among his peers Brian is considered one of the stars of their Biddy Basketball league. But his skill pales in comparison to his brother's.

As Marty is named most valuable player in the conference and leads his team to victory after victory, Holly and Scott are on the sidelines at every game. They shout encouragement, but most often directions, from the stands, and boast to their friends about their son the star. Marty feels that his excellence in sports is the one thing that earns him his parents' approval, so he becomes singularly focused on winning. He hogs the ball during games and viciously criticizes teammates who make mistakes. He scorns his brother's efforts, calling him "little league."

Eventually Brian drops out of basketball. Holly and Scott, so wrapped up in Marty's success, barely notice. His parents' drive to always win has resulted in Brian's abandonment. Their lack of acknowledgment of his efforts has damaged his self-esteem and driven him to despair of ever gaining their approval. Brian has begun to feel, What's the use of trying? That despair and depression have begun to seep into other areas of his life. Meanwhile, Marty has become ruthless in his efforts to be number one in every area. Being the best at all he does has become his mission, and when he's failed on occasion, he's been devastated.

As a parent, you need to find each child's strengths and praise him for that. Learn to praise children for the effort, not the accomplishment. Let them know you value their working to their fullest potential. You don't value your child because she has excelled but because of the effort she expended. You want your children to compete against themselves rather than each other, to work toward their own personal best.

Holly and Scott, in their failure to teach the boys how to handle losses and disappointment, have done them a great disservice. Kids need to know they won't always win. In order to grow a loving family, you need to emphasize that there's fun in the challenge and in getting better. Losing is okay if you put in your best effort.

Kids can learn to analyze what they did and the benefits of practicing. You can impart that everyone learns from mistakes, that they're not to be avoided and feared. Instead, mistakes are a natural part of learning.

It's also imperative for you to overcome any feelings of favoritism you may feel toward any one of your children. Perhaps the worst damage Holly and Scott have caused Brian was demonstrating their lack of interest in his feelings and his life experiences. Such behavior is a form of emotional abuse in the form of neglect. It's your responsibility as a parent never to hurt your children in this way. If you feel you're unable to stop this behavior, either because of problems in your current life or because of past experiences, we urge you to seek professional help immediately, for your child's sake as well as your own.

Holly and Scott are beginning to acknowledge their problem after years of denial. It's a start, and the greater their insight and awareness, the better the prognosis for both of their sons to develop positive self-esteem and sibling relationships.

Embrace Your Stepchildren

When stepsiblings enter the family dynamics, as is increasingly the case as divorced parents remarry, sibling rivalry enters a whole new category. A common issue is loyalty to biological siblings, which may cause children to team up against each other. Stepsiblings need to develop their own relationship. It cannot be forced on them by parents anxious for their blended family to get along. Age-appropriate activities and outings are the best way to foster communication. Trips to amusement parks and sporting and music events are interactive activities that are conducive to getting along. (Though we don't mean to imply that all family activities need to be extravagant. A board game at home can work just as well.) Work together with your new spouse to make sure the children know they're not expected to have the same level of intimacy and closeness they have with their biological siblings and that this is not only normal but okay.

Building a relationship takes time. Insist that the children show respect for one another. Do not allow hostility. Explain and model the communication techniques we discussed in Chapter 3 as a framework for resolving conflicts. Discuss and allow open expression of feelings regarding sharing their biological parent with stepsiblings. It's typical that as the stepparent attempts to form a bond with his stepchild, his biological child will feel displaced and resentful. This is a perfect opportunity for team-spirited interaction to be modeled by both parents.

Eleven Ways to Strengthen the Sibling Bond

1. In a family in which there's a new child, you want to make sure that the older sibling doesn't feel displaced or dethroned, no longer special. Include your child in the process of welcoming the new baby, and even in the pregnancy.

2. To foster communication among siblings in their early years, you can develop a behavior chart—using stickers that depict the children's positive interactions and cooperative behavior.

3. To highlight the importance of cooperation, you can build projects into their daily schedules that require cooperation.

4. You can help your children develop alliance and unity by letting them help you plan their brother's birthday party. When they're older, give them a task that they have to figure out how to accomplish together, like rearranging their shared toys.

5. Within the context of competition, children should be encouraged to support each other's achievements. It's good to involve each child in developing her sibling's strengths. If one child is interested in tennis, you can involve the other child in picking out something like a good luck charm to encourage and motivate her so she can feel a part of her sibling's success.

6. It's also good for siblings to observe each other handling successes and disappointments and to be involved in that process. One sibling can provide reassurance to the other.

7. Sometimes siblings can develop an interest in the same sport or activity. That can be turned into a plus as the more skilled sibling can provide leadership and role modeling. The key to nipping the rivalry aspect is making sure they have a positive

relationship—that they're talking, interacting, and involved with each other in a positive way.

8. Engage children in the process of developing a positive relationship. Have your children talk about their feelings together. Express how important it is, for instance, to ask first if you want to borrow a toy.

9. Let them tell you their perceptions of their relationship including their views of the amount of bickering they do. At the same time, have them identify when things are going well, too. Keep in mind that for children, the appeal of fighting is the excitement and stimulation it brings and, yet, doesn't portend a lifetime of hatred.

10. Ask them what they fight about most and strategize together to find a compromise. Give them opportunities to grow in their conflict resolution and ownership of the solution to the problem, not just what you see as the problem. Communicate with them between fights.

11. Have your children make a list of what they love best (and least) about their siblings so you can assess as a family where the problems lie. Jealousy and envy are normal, so you should impress upon your children that it's okay to feel it but not okay to act it out physically or with verbal abuse.

Living the Sixth Principle

Learn to give to your children according to their needs, even when all of your children can't see what they need. Allow them to express their dissatisfaction, yet remain firm in your decisions.

No sibling relationship is ever perfect. But when you and your partner work as a team to nurture the sibling bond, confronting conflicts head-on, not only will you prevent sibling rivalry from becoming emotionally and physically damaging, you will produce positive results from that rivalry.

Many of the skills you teach your children about communicating and relating to their siblings will be the very same skills they need to thrive in their outside environment.

7

Acknowledge Peer Pressure: The Seventh Principle

Taking time to know my children's friends is important to me and will enhance my relationship with my children. I will extend myself yet allow my children space and greater independence as they mature.

Siblings may be your child's first playmates, but once she begins school, her world opens up to a lifetime of peer relations—and the accompanying roller coaster ride. Your child will laugh with her peers and be hurt by them as well, often in the same play date. The ups and downs she negotiates will teach her valuable lessons about surviving in her childhood world and beyond.

It's through her peers that she'll learn who she is as an individual apart from her parents. In the learning there will be much joy you can celebrate and much pain from which you need to console her. Because along with peer relations comes peer pressure. Acknowledging that pressure in your child's life will help you to help her grow.

The Power of Peer Pressure

All parents want their children to have friends. Yet few of us are prepared for the forceful influence peer pressure will have on our child's life. The first time your child comes home in tears because she "doesn't fit in" since she can't stay up as late as all her friends can is the first time that all the care and thought you've put into raising your child will be challenged by people who are significantly shorter and younger—and presumably less knowledgeable about parenting—than you are.

At the same time, it's completely necessary for a child's development. As children mature, their need for self-discovery increases. They go through the transition of being influenced primarily by you to being socially involved with friends. They're seeking to become their own person and learning to express their emotions. Peer relationships help them to develop their self-image and their self-esteem.

All children want to belong to a peer group, but promoting the social-skill development they need to do so is your task. You have to teach children to get along, communicate, share, and engage in social activities. They evolve from little people at parallel play to bigger people who enjoy interactive games and activities. Parents need to guide that growth. You need to help children understand the rules of fair play, monitoring, and intervening when necessary.

You also need to teach them how to get along with others. This requires being courteous, saying please and thank you at home, long before their journey into the outside world. They can practice during phone calls to family members. Help them engage in conversations with Grandma, for instance.

It's important to help your child handle her feelings of discomfort so she can be successful with social skills. Some children feel anxious when they meet new people, so you can help them by letting them practice with people they already feel comfortable greeting.

We used to use cue cards for Dottie when she was six, because we realized that when she spoke with her godfather Marvin on the telephone, she was unable to think of what to say. She was quite comfortable speaking to him in person, but, as it does for many children, speaking on the phone made her nervous. The cue cards reminded her to tell him about school, her teacher, her projects, and the like.

Many parents who are shy want their children to be gregarious. But if you want your children to be outgoing, you have to model that. Make sure your child actually uses words when he meets people and doesn't simply rely on nodding his head. He needs to become at ease with the idea of communicating with others. This will be hard for him if he's not outgoing, but with practice and time he'll learn to overcome his fears.

Whatever example you set, your children will almost surely follow. For instance, we have taught our children that whenever there's a guest in our home, we must stop what we're doing and greet that person. Yet one day Derek, anxious and intent on putting groceries away, headed straight toward the kitchen without acknowledging that good friends of ours had just arrived from out of town and were sitting in our living room. Dottie and D.J. have not yet let him forget that.

How Peer Pressure Starts

Now that children attend day care and preschool, peer pressure begins much earlier than you might expect. A big issue in modern society is materialism, which emerges as soon as children are old enough to understand TV commercials, usually around preschool age. Suddenly they feel the need to have what everyone else has. You may start to feel that your family value system is being compromised. You can teach your children that there's nothing wrong with having nice things but that material items shouldn't be a measure of their self-esteem.

No parents want their child to feel out of place, but it's important to talk to your child about what it really means to them to have the latest brand of sneakers. Once you know where they stand, your decision is an individual one that fits into your family budget. The idea is to fall somewhere between the extreme of never letting your child have what others have and always letting him have whatever he asks for.

Be aware, too, if your child says he wants the latest Pokémon cards and you run out to spend hundreds of dollars on them, are you fulfilling his desires or your own? Were you denied all that you thought you "had to have" as a child? If so, you may be trying to satisfy your own needs more than your child's need to fit in.

Peer pressure also exposes your children to different values and lifestyles that challenge your own. For instance, some families don't object to violent television programming. And as a result, some of their children have difficulty understanding how unacceptable aggressive behavior can be. When our son was starting school, other boys acted out Power Rangers, a TV show he was not as familiar with but soon developed some curiosity about. While D.J. had increasing interest, he didn't display any preference for acting out scenes by kicking and yelling as several of his peers did. Instead, he collected a few of the toys that, when properly arranged, transformed into complex objects like futuristic cars, trucks, and planes. His interest in Power Rangers gradually faded, while his friends' interest seemed to increase.

This example illustrates that a child's temperament can also determine how much influence his peers will have on him. If he doesn't show a tendency toward or interest in aggressive behavior, it's likely he'll be less influenced by aggressive examples.

Susceptibility to peer pressure is also greater when a child is vulnerable because of other situations, like the death of a close family member, a sudden and serious threat or loss such as divorce, harsh sibling abuse, or financial difficulties, among other things. Due to situations such as these, parental involvement may be lower than usual and frustration higher, making the child feel more reliant on peers for support he ordinarily could get from his parents.

Mindy began to come home late from cheerleading practice. At first her mother, Sela, just let it go with a reminder to be on time. Sela had been a bit preoccupied with her son. Jake had made the travel soccer team and was having trouble balancing homework and other responsibilities. Sela was proud of his effort and tried to make every game.

One evening Mindy was over an hour late coming in, and when Sela questioned her, she became defiant and stated that all her friends hang out for a while after practice. Sela threatened to start picking Mindy up if she couldn't come straight home. Mindy continued to be late. One evening Sela decided to go to practice. When she arrived, she found out that Mindy had been leaving practice early, using the excuse that her parents said she had too much homework. When confronted, Mindy disclosed that she had been going to a friend's house where other youth "hung out" and watched talk shows.

Sela was relieved that she and Mindy were able to talk. Although there was tension and anger, Sela recognized that Mindy had been vulnerable because of the changes in the family's routine and the decrease in her attention and involvement with Mindy. This didn't excuse Mindy's behavior, but it helped Sela understand it. Although she punished Mindy, Sela also knew what she had to do differently. She made herself available in the evenings more often and showed more interest in Mindy's interests and activities. Sela also allowed some of Mindy's friends to come to their house after school on occasion, a gesture Mindy appreciated.

In most cases when children act out peer pressure–related behavior, they're merely testing you to see how you'll react. A preschool child who observes a playmate defy a parent's authority by refusing to put away toys may be curious to know what will happen if he emulates this behavior with you. A grade-school child might "talk back" after witnessing his friend yell at his parent to see if he can get away with it. By adolescence, however, his susceptibility to pressure to engage in sex, drink alcohol, or cut school will have less to do with your reaction — unless he's seeking your attention, which needs to be examined further before he's hurt — and more to do with how much he understands the consequences of yielding to peer pressure.

You shouldn't overreact when children emulate a behavior you don't approve of. A strong reaction of alarm on your part will shut down communication from your child, who may have wanted to talk about it. If your child returned from a social situation behaving differently, would you be prepared to talk to her? Imagine your reaction. Think about how you would begin the dialogue.

Peer relationships can reveal a great deal about your child's sense of self-esteem and personality development and can be beneficial to her. They provide children with the opportunity to learn how to express their individuality and to have a sense of identification. "I wear jeans like the other girls do, but I prefer black to blue jeans." "I like Pokémon like the rest of my class, but I don't enjoy trading my cards." Whenever your child expresses individuality and withstands peer pressure, support her. Foster her confidence in developing her own individual strengths, pointing out how strong she is not to give in to pressures.

Recognizing whether your child is an independent thinker and leader or more of a conformist and follower will help you determine the degree of power peer pressure will have on her.

Are you prepared to help your child to face peer pressure? The answer depends in part on how you answer the following questions, whether *Most Often*, *Sometimes*, or *Seldom*. The more times you say *Most Often*, the better:

- Do you usually take note of any changes in her behavior and ask her about how she's doing in general?

- Do you spend time with your child so you can guide him through social situations that seem to make him uncomfortable?

- Have you developed trust in her appropriate to her age and maturity?

- Do you encourage honesty? (Though once he's a teenager, don't expect to learn all the details of his life.)

- Do you make sure she understands consequences?

- Does he know that he will always be loved by you, but some of his behavior will be challenged by you and others?

Handling Peer Pressure at Every Age

There are differences in psychological and developmental stages that necessitate different parental approaches to peer pressure. Infants and toddlers have friends who are children of their parents' friends or associates. At this point parents have direct influence over whom their children form attachments and relationships with. Most often if you view your child's playmates as having a negative impact, you'll reduce the number of times the children get together, or you'll stop contact altogether.

But children have a greater psychological drive toward independence and autonomy as they develop. Suddenly there are others in their lives whose opinions they want to hear. Your grade-school child will develop interests that are directed toward peer acceptance and approval, gaining social skills, hobbies, extracurricular activities, and athletic achievement. She will get feedback and guidance from other adult authority figures such as teachers and coaches.

Negative and positive peer pressures are incorporated into the grade-school child's system of justice and fairness. The media, school, religious training, and outside activities all influence how he relates to peers. Peer pressure can work to your advantage, too. Peer influence can sometimes inspire and motivate each other to reach honor roll status, for instance. It can help your child to participate in a healthy activity, such as volunteerism, or a club he might not have thought to join on his own. In a classroom of students divided into two teams for a spelling bee, peers can work together to cheer each other on. In these ways the peer pressure your school-age child experiences will be to his benefit.

At this point, too, whatever result peer pressure yields, you still have the freedom of the final say. You can tell your child that you'll always listen to her, that you'll always hear her express her desires and interests, and that you want to hear her input, but you still have the right to make the decisions. Don't be surprised, however, if your child accuses you of not listening because you're not giving her the answer she wants to hear! You can say, "I may not be agreeing, but I am listening."

The adolescent is dealing with hormonal and physical growth during puberty. This can be a turbulent developmental stage for both parents and teenager, as we discussed in Principle Five. Adolescents have a great desire to demonstrate their autonomy and independence. Peers are simply more important to them than their parents are. This can be painful for you, but there's a right way and a wrong way to handle it.

Some parents attempt to control and limit their child's need for greater independence. But the focus should be to guide your child to become his own person and function independently in society. We cannot protect teens from ever making mistakes and experiencing the reality of the world.

Compared to preschool and grade-school children, teenagers want less of our time, attention, guidance, and companionship. However, there are times when they need it more than younger children. They seek out peers and love interests, through crushes or dating experiences. These relationships tend to come and go, and exploring these different friendships helps teens determine what qualities are necessary for long-term relationships. You can talk with them about your experiences, including challenges and struggles as a way to maintain a connection. Keep in mind, too, that often while teens are protesting your intrusion into their lives with one side of their mouth, they're expressing gratitude for your involvement with the other. Studies show they really do want your involvement—on their terms—because it shows them how much you care about them.

The Gender Factor

Most of us recognize that peer pressure has the potential for a negative result more often than not. But your children will be hard-pressed to see it that way at times. Not long ago Dot had a painful experience with peer pressure that involved two other girls. The other two had been close friends, but one day one of them called Dot and started pretending to be her good friend while bad-mouthing the other girl. We tried to warn Dot that this didn't sound right to us and that we didn't think it right that this girl was mistreating someone she had formerly called a friend. Yet Dot kept telling us we were wrong about her. Dot, who was innocent of the dynamics at play, became vulnerable to the pressure of ignoring the other girl. But because this was outwardly hurting one little girl, the teacher finally got involved. It came to light that the girl who was doing the ostracizing was reacting to what she had felt was a slight of her. Dot got caught in the middle. She now tells us with great surprise that we were right.

Like you, when it comes to social situations like these, we'd rather have been wrong. None of us want to see our child hurt or manipulated by others. However, although we were concerned with the incident, we were pleased with Dot's openness and communication with us.

Unfortunately, as much as we dislike stereotypes, it does seem to play out that the scenario above is far more common among girls than boys. Girls, raised to be social beings, are often encouraged to develop verbal communication skills, which is a good thing. The downside is that sometimes in group situations that same skill in relating can turn to verbal manipulation and insults. On the other hand, boys are often socialized and expected to be more physical, direct, and abrupt in their communication style. Consequently, they are more likely to engage in physical confrontations and aggression.

Dealing with Prejudice and Interracial Friendships

Most of us raise our children to be accepting of differences. But when they enter school and hear their best friend put down a child of a different skin color, they can become confused. If this girl they like to play with at recess doesn't like that Muslim girl, she's probably right, right? Or they come home making comments you've never heard from them before, like "Monique has really funny hair with lots of beads in it. I don't want to play with her" or "Erica doesn't want Cathy to be in our club because she isn't black."

When your child appears to be demonstrating prejudice or discriminating against other children, you may be disappointed or frustrated, and feel challenged as to how to handle it. But you can counteract your child's newfound prejudice by exposing him to diversity and modeling cross-race friendships and interacting with people from various backgrounds. Don't ridicule him or punish him for what he's said. Instead, hear him out, and then be open about your perceptions. Encourage free-flowing communication. Your child should be able to express his opinions and experiences without feeling condemned. Continue with an open discussion that clearly states your values and views. Prejudicial behaviors and insults should not be tolerated, but you should acknowledge for your child that not everyone will share your family values on this issue. Discuss ways he can handle his peers when this occurs. Open discussion of feelings will lead to greater understanding and problem solving.

Still, peer pressure can be brutal on this topic. We've known of children—boys and girls—who have been in a sense ambushed when they surpass their peers, particularly when it comes to grades. It seems as though you're not allowed to be smarter or do better than your peer group. This has particularly been an issue for African Americans, who in some cases have been accused of selling out, of adopting a white person's values, as though education belonged to one race only. In many cases white children have been ostracized when they have black or Latino friends, because others have difficulties with interracial friendships.

In our book *Raising the Rainbow Generation* we note that in this generation America is moving rapidly toward becoming the most culturally, racially, and ethnically diverse nation in the world. It is clear that all children need to learn about the accomplishments and achievements of diverse cultures in order to be prepared to live in this multicultural society of the near future. Diversity occurs not only across groups but even within a particular group, so children also need to be taught that neither all blacks nor all whites nor other groups speak alike or engage in the same cultural practices to the same extent.

Peer influence can exert unreasonable pressure for your child to treat others who are different in a prejudiced or discriminatory manner. Your child may need your support in exploring friendships beyond his immediate peer group.

You can model openness to diversity by encouraging and joining your child's journey to learning about others of different cultural backgrounds. Cross-cultural acquaintances and friendships provide living examples of appreciating and celebrating diversity. Neighbors, co-workers, teachers, community leaders, and local business owners are a readily available resource for fostering multicultural awareness and acceptance in your child.

Teaching our children to develop positive peer relationships with people from different racial and cultural backgrounds helps them to have greater understanding and an acceptance of differences. It enriches their experiences and helps them learn how to relate and interact. It also gives them leadership potential in dealing with racial conflicts. In order for peer pressure to loosen its grip on our children, we all need to be more open.

Dealing with Sex

You may not like to talk about it, but peers expose your children to ideas and awareness of sex, violence, and aggression. The more your child feels comfortable talking to you about these subjects, the less confusion peers will be able to create for her.

> Dara remembers being in the bathroom at her Catholic high school and hearing the term "blow job" for the first time and not knowing what it meant. Because her mother had consistently told her, "Ask me anything," and had followed through by remaining calm and responsive when Dara approached her with questions, Dara couldn't wait to ask her mom. Although her mom now

admits to often feeling overwhelmed and uncomfortable, Dara
always perceived her mother as approachable. Her mother
explained, appropriately without specific detail, what the girls in
the bathroom were referring to. Although Dara was flabbergasted,
she was pleased that her mother informed her.

Talking about sex with your children prepares them to deal with peer discussions. You should always transmit your values, and this includes feelings and thoughts about love, intimacy, and commitment. Talk to your children about their bodies as early as preschool age, and use books to describe private parts with proper names. By grade school, read more advanced books together that focus on how babies are made. This is the time when your child should have basic information. Then you can increase the discussion based on your child's questions and curiosity.

But puberty, a time of raging hormones and physical changes—which increasingly is beginning as early as age ten for girls—is a crucial time for reinforcing respect for one's body and also for others. Young men need to focus on peer relationships and how they feel about young women. You need to have conversations with your son that counteracts misogynistic influences and discussions among peers. You can expect—and remember—that some exploration of sexual urges will occur. Often there's pressure from peers for your child to demonstrate an ability to attract the opposite sex.

Your discussions with your child shouldn't focus only on the mechanics and biology of sex but on the emotional and spiritual aspects as well. Teaching your child that positive peer relationships don't include pressure to engage in premature sex is a challenge and responsibility. Teaching them the value of emotional closeness and trust in friendships is the key. But when teenagers are sexually active or at risk of becoming so, you also need to teach them the proper use of a condom and educate them about sexually transmitted diseases.

Dealing with Violence and Aggression

Anger is a normal human emotion, and your task is to teach children to express it appropriately. But in our society, in which examples of violence seem to dominate our media, it's normal for you to fear not only for your child's safety but for her ability to handle aggression as well.

Developmentally, preschool children will lash out physically at peers when they're angry because they don't have verbal skills to express their anger. Your child may also be subjected to aggression from a playmate. Help him to label his anger as a feeling and teach him to say, "I feel angry when . . . " Begin this as early as preschool. Intervene and guide your child's peer in this process, too, if the friend is in your care and interacting with your child.

When your child is in grade school, monitor and direct how she handles anger. If she talks about violence as a way to resolve her conflicts, deal with this firmly and directly—whether she's the perpetrator or victim. If she expresses fantasies of retaliation or vindictive behavior, talk openly about her feelings and problem-solve other approaches. The very act of validating her feelings will help her not to react. If you fail to do so and she internalizes her anger, this can lead to an explosive episode, as well as to a general lack of impulse control.

After the shootings at the Columbine High School, most parents are even more concerned about violence. If you see any early warning signs, like sudden withdrawal or expressions of hatred, deal with them immediately. Many kids resort to physical confrontations when they're provoked by insults from peers. They often think they have to stand up for themselves and prove they're not intimidated. Teach your adolescent that he can protect himself by being verbal and remaining in control, and that doing so is a sign of his strength. Instruct him about alternatives to violence, like walking away, backing off, apologizing, seeking help, and agreeing to disagree. You can even encourage your child to approach conflict with a spirit of being a "peacemaker" among his peers.

Separating Out Your Feelings from Your Child's Feelings

It's not surprising that as parents we view peer pressure as a negative influence on our children, one that interferes with our authority and guidance. But your feelings can go beyond this as well, in fact, back into your own past. Your past experiences with peer pressure can affect your children.

If you remember experiences in which peers influenced you, it is likely you'll be hypersensitive, if not overly protective of your child in this area. For example, you may recall that during a sleepover in fifth grade your friends tried smoking cigarettes, drinking, or sexual play. Maybe it was even something more severe, like drugs, or less severe, like calling a girl and hanging up. These experiences may make you overcompensate with your child. You may look for these behaviors or problems when they don't yet exist—still there are times when a child senses a parent's lack of trust, and self-sabotages, as in, "Why not? She already thinks I'm doing it."

If parents are accusatory and negative, children sometimes rebel, or parental comments become a self-fulfilling prophecy. If a child continuously hears that he's a troublemaker, he'll be at risk for acting like a troublemaker. Some parents think that reverse psychology may work. They think that if you say, "You won't amount to anything," your child will see it as a challenge and do the opposite. We don't believe in this approach. A challenge should be presented as such and be perceived by your child as motivation and incentive, not discouragement or criticism. For example, "You do so well. I know you can do even better."

If you recognize that you're being overprotective, it's a good first step. Awareness is critical. You then must move toward more openness and flexibility. Be honest with your child that you want to protect him, and the more you trust that he understands your values and shows good judgment, the more flexible you can be. Your goal is to guide your child to make good decisions about peer pressure. You don't want to see your child hurt. Who does? We didn't want Dot to experience being manipulated. But that's not realistic. At some point, after you've given them a clear sense of your values and helped them to brainstorm how they can handle a situation in a self-enhancing rather than a self-defeating way, you have to step back and let children experience it.

Another problem parents may have with peer pressure is that they may react more strongly than warranted to their child's social problems. Watching your child experience some of the downsides of peer pressure, like being in the "out" group, shunned by the "in" group, or ridiculed for not being able to afford the expensive sneakers of other peers, can cause you to feel pain for your child. But it can also awaken painful memories of your own peer situations as a child.

Overidentifying with your child can be harmful to her, because what she's experiencing may not be as painful to her. It's important for you to recognize what's triggering this reaction for you and not pass it on to your child. Why put problems and concerns in her head that don't exist for her?

Most of us have wanted to intervene and maybe even "shake the daylights" out of a peer who has physically or emotionally assaulted our child. These protective instincts are natural. However, good sense usually tells us that our children need to learn how to negotiate conflict and handle problems with our guidance more than our intervention. Not only does our intervention rob them of the opportunity to gain confidence in managing problems; it can also make their situation worse.

Noelle recalls that when she was a child, her father would run to her defense every time a neighborhood bully teased her. He would threaten to tell the boy's father, who, it turned out, didn't care. The result was that Noelle was teased unmercifully as soon as her father wasn't with her. Over time Noelle learned to deal with it on her own, never telling her father that his "help" had made a bad situation much worse for her.

Of course, there are times when you must intervene. But most often what your children need most is your support, your listening ear, and your suggestions. If your children are being negatively influenced, you also need to be able to listen, compromise when necessary, guide, and set clear limits when appropriate. The challenge is differentiating between times when you need to be firm and times when you need to be flexible. Some things should be nonnegotiable in families, like drug experimentation. Other things should be rules that are negotiable, like bedtime or curfew. Still other things should be flexible, like scheduling activities with friends.

1. Do you know most of your child's friends?

2. Does your child enjoy bringing his friends to your home?

3. Does your child have a very different view of his friends than you do?

4. Do you spend time with your child's friends?

5. Does your child emulate friends' behaviors that you disapprove of?

6. Does your child have friends whom you view as a very positive influence?

7. Do you intervene when your child has a conflict with a peer?

8. Does your worry or concern become unbearable when your child visits or spends time away from home?

9. Do you trust your child's judgment when he is relating to peers independent of you?

10. Do you attempt to control whom your child spends time with?

This inventory will assist you in identifying areas that may create stress or difficulty. If you answered no to questions 1, 2, 3, 4, 6, and

9 and yes to questions 5, 7, 8, and 10, then there are areas to explore and work through. It's important to know your child's friends and make your home a welcoming environment. If your child views his friends differently than you do, respect your child enough to get to know his friends before passing judgment. This will show your child that you want to understand him.

If there are things that are totally unacceptable, this should be stated clearly and firmly. However, if your impression is vague and without any solid information or facts, your child will resent it and possibly rebel. More important, your distrust doesn't create a family dynamic of openness and honesty.

If your child is emulating behaviors that are unacceptable to you, you should address the behavior and not the person. Be clear and specific in your feedback. Friends who are a positive influence certainly will make you feel more secure, but be careful not to make comparisons or pressure your child to conform. The process should be natural and mutual.

Children should be allowed time to handle problems themselves. Then parents should guide them. But if the problem is excessive or persistent, parents should intervene. Children need guidance and mediation at times.

If you're worried when your child is away, this is normal. However, any excessive monitoring or concern means that the environment might not be the best or that you're being overprotective. Process this with your partner in parenting and your support team.

Parental intuition shouldn't be taken lightly. If you're usually able to allow your child autonomy and a degree of independence but feel uncertain about a certain event, follow your intuition.

Trusting your child's judgment depends on the foundation you have established. Your goal should be to move from control to trust along with reasonable supervision.

Teaching Your Child about Friendship and Fitting In

From as early as their preschool years, children understand the value of friendship and want nothing more than to be liked and to fit in. As a parent, you have to help them to learn the social skills that make this possible, beyond the basic courtesy we mentioned earlier.

The first time you take them to a library program or dance class, help them learn to introduce themselves to other children. Some children are more spontaneous than others and will share all the details of their home life in their first introductory breath, while others hang back, preferring to scan the room before entering the group. Help your child to seek out those whose interests are similar to his own. Teach him that you do this by talking about your interests, hobbies, and experiences. As children talk to one another, they find out what they have in common. Identifying these similarities opens the door for shared experiences. You can guide your child by asking, "Does Hank play the piano or soccer like you? Does Shelly take gymnastics or swimming lessons?" Setting up play dates is a way to observe how children interact—if they get along well, share similar interests, and enjoy each other's company.

Role-play with your child what he can do before each new situation until he's comfortable interacting without your help. Over time, children will gravitate toward those children with whom they're most comfortable. Their choices might occasionally make you wince, such as when your quiet, introspective child seeks out the class troublemaker. Chances are, in this case your child is drawn to a personality characteristic he unconsciously wishes he had. Sometimes these friendships can be enduring as each fulfills a need for the other; other times it can be an experiment that will eventually lose its attraction for your child.

Help your children understand that so often when someone tries something new, like a friendship, it may not work out, and that's okay. Support them when they express their individuality in peer situations, helping them to see that eventually, they'll become more confident with their values.

Understand, too, that there is an ebb and flow to peer pressure, depending upon your child's age. The toddler doesn't much care whom he plays with, as long as the other child has interesting toys. The school-age child wants both conformity and adult approval, while the adolescent wants individuality. When you understand this, you can help them to better grasp the dynamics of friendship and fitting in.

Guiding Children toward More Positive Relationships

Eight-year-old Theo and his friend Jamal were teasing a classmate while getting off the school bus. Theo's mom, Dee, heard him call the other boy a sissy. When she talked to Theo, he said that Jamal had said it first. Dee was clear with Theo that his behavior was inappropriate and hurtful. Theo agreed to apologize to his classmate. When Jamal came over to play later, Dee talked to the two boys together. Jamal was embarrassed and remorseful. He, too, agreed to apologize.

If you discover that peers are engaging in behavior that is inappropriate or nonnegotiable to you, you should set explicit limits and boundaries with your child. Make your disapproval and concerns clear. Be direct in indicating what's unacceptable and why the behavior is wrong. If need be, you can tell them they can't play together for a period of time. If later you assess that you overreacted or took too strong a stance, you can reassess and renegotiate. This is particularly true with teens. When dealing with adolescents, be sure to use open communication and compromise.

At the same time, with effort on your part, you can steer them toward relationships that are more positive. If your child connects well with a girl who shares her interest in playing the piano and putting on home plays, make an effort to arrange more frequent play dates for them. It's important that you let your child be with children who have a good influence on her. It's a bit harder to do so with adolescents, but you can extend yourself more, being available as chauffeur, for instance, so the friends can be together.

Relating to Your Child's Friends

It's important to get to know your child's friends, and spending time with them is the best way to do so. Offer to take the friends on an outing. Volunteer in your child's classroom. This gives you an opportunity to see how your child and her friend think, relate, and influence one another.

You can and should monitor your child's friendships without taking over. You want to be sure friendships are going well and that overall there's a positive influence. If you have any concerns, discuss them in a nonjudgmental and open manner. Be specific about any perceived difficulties, and identify what's troubling you. Help your children learn how to make good judgments and decisions. Guide this process without making them for them.

You want to make your home welcoming to your children's friends. Invite your children's friends over to your house, and really get to know them. Provide snacks and activities that they're interested in, like computer games. This gives you an opportunity to engage in conversation with them, observe your children's and their friends' interactions and offer guidance. The friends will get to know you, too, and understand what your expectations are.

We have an open-door policy with our children regarding their friends. As long as one of us is home and it's not a family-only day, our children are allowed to have friends over. Further, as long as toys and other items are put away before the friends go home, our children are allowed to play freely with dress-up clothes and games and to play music to dance to. Our children's friends enjoy our house, and we both are comfortable with these children because we have frequent opportunities to get to know them.

How to Talk about Peer Pressure with Your Child

At some point your child will have questions about peer pressure, from how to handle a situation he's experiencing to one he sees a friend going through. Short of doing what you most desire—being there to take care of it for him—the most realistic and fairest approach in order to nurture your child's independence is to give him the tools to handle pressures on his own.

We recommend you start with a "what if?" discussion. Here's how it goes: You ask your child "what if?" and then describe a scenario to him and ask him how he would handle it. Listen to how he problem-solves, and give him some ideas when he needs your support. For example:

> Mom: What if your friend offered you a cigarette?
>
> Son: I'd tell him that I don't think it's cool to smoke.

That's a fine answer for a boy who we'll assume knows that your family value is that smoking is not healthy. This example also illustrates the point that you must encourage your children to be vigilant when they see trouble coming and learn how to handle it.

But if you have a child who seems socially challenged, so that every answer to your "what if?" game indicates he just doesn't understand how to help himself in social situations, you'll have to go beyond an open-ended approach to help him comprehend what the consequences of his suggestions could be. Say, "I understand what you're saying, but what do you think would happen if you did that?" You have to teach your child insight and judgment. Help him to see what could be a problem for him. He's a child who won't benefit from the open-ended "what if?" but could use a multiple-choice lesson. For example:

> Mom: What if your friend asked you to hide Sally's schoolbooks? Would you do what he said? Would you tell him, "No way"? Or would you tell your teacher?

This approach takes a bit more time, but your child will benefit from your input and eventually will learn that there are many different ways to handle peer pressures.

However, when your child is the victim of ridicule by her peers, she shouldn't be expected to handle it on her own. Parental intervention is important in order to help your child cope with her school life. Particularly if she has special needs, you'll want to protect her as much as you can. What seems to work well in school settings as children have become mainstreamed is the development of the buddy system, whereby a child who is identified by a teacher as having special needs is partnered with the mainstreamed child. Children enjoy this opportunity to help others, and the buddy system is usually seen as a positive relationship.

But the one thing you need to emphasize to your child repeatedly is that she should never suffer in silence. She should seek out an adult who can guide her through the peer problem and then the adult should step back and let her handle it. We know that children intuitively understand that when they become "snitches," their social problem will only get worse. But they need to be helped to see that coming to you is not snitching. You can inform the teacher that there is a problem that he or she needs to watch out for. Then he or she can observe it personally and address the entire class. No one need ever know it was through your child that the problem became identified.

When it's your child who's joining in the put-downs, teach her to have more empathy, and help her understand the impact that her behavior is having on the picked-on person. She has to understand that what's popular isn't always right and what's right isn't always popular.

But in all peer pressure situations, you and your child have to keep it in perspective. Children will often think that whatever social crisis they're experiencing at the moment is the end of their life. It becomes such a major issue and feels overwhelming to them. They don't realize how blessed they are. Teach them to think rationally, that though this is painful, it's not a catastrophe. Help them to see that tomorrow is a new day and that what feels awful today will pass in time. Help them to be forgiving of themselves. And don't forget to say, "I still love you."

Giving Your Child Basic Communication Tools

How can you guide your child to express his feelings in healthy ways? Here are some techniques that will help you.

- For the preschool child, begin by labeling his feelings. Children need to be able to say when they're feeling sad, angry, happy, and so on.

- For grade-school children, begin to have conversations about feelings. These children are becoming skilled verbally and so can naturally increase their ability to express their feelings. They can be guided in learning to elaborate and discuss feelings and make connections to underlying issues and antecedents. For example, "When X happened, I felt . . . because . . ." A child who has had a conflict with a peer can say, "When Chad didn't invite me to his party, I felt angry, because I thought we were friends and he left me out. I also feel disappointed and sad."

- Help children to set limits and boundaries with their peers. Help them to sort out what treatment they will and will not tolerate from others. This will enhance self-esteem.

- Help adolescents by discussing what type of adults they want to become.

- Help teens express feelings about whom they want to open up to and what type of friendships they want to have with different people. Guiding this process involves modeling it for them and maintaining open communication with them.

- Go back to Chapter 3 to refresh your memory about the Seven Golden Rules of Communication.

When You Should Worry

Though parents dread it, normal rebellion by teenagers is expected. However, if it's excessive, your teen may be emulating her peers. If her behavior has changed dramatically, this could mean that her peers are negatively influencing her. Some youth talk openly about being hostile and belligerent with parents. Disrespect and anger are seen as being "cool" and independent, but you should be concerned.

You should be concerned, too, if you don't know who the peers are that are troubling your teen, and she's unwilling to share that information. If there's something your child has enjoyed and she suddenly refuses to do it, that's a red flag, too.

> Chelsea's usually polite daughter, Tia, enjoyed tennis lessons, but suddenly one afternoon on her way to lessons, she copped an attitude with Chelsea. Surprised, Chelsea tried to draw Tia out and finally discovered that Tia's classmates were teasing her about tennis lessons and trying to get her to quit and join their basketball team, which held practice the same time. Tia was ready to give in to them to fit in, but she was conflicted about it, and it showed in how she treated Chelsea.

Finally, if there has been deterioration in your communication with your child and conflicts arise when you do try to communicate, you should also be concerned. Determine what's going on and begin to help your child to see what led to this situation. Help her to see the consequences of her actions and to process that knowledge. If your child has an attitude with you, you can stop her and point out how her treatment of you is making you feel and encourage her to tell you what's wrong. It is your expression of parental love that counts, but your children should know the limits and boundaries regarding what they may and may not say to you when they're upset.

Throughout the many peer situations that can arise for your child, there will be times when you may be too emotional or subjective to handle a situation. Being able to depend on your support system of family, friends, and community is critical when you need an objective opinion. In some cases you may want to seek professional help. If your child refuses professional help, a trusted friend, family member, or clergyperson may be beneficial. Finding someone your child trusts is of utmost importance.

How to Handle Passing Fads

Fortunately, most of what your child will experience of the world of peer pressure will be a passing fad. If your fourteen-year-old daughter seems drawn to peers who put streaks in their hair and she wants to, you may want to be flexible here. The usual anxiety is, If they want to do this what will be next? Choose your battles and the areas that are cause for real concern. Understanding that this, too, shall pass, once you've determined that it's not harmful to your child, might help you to let it go.

But for the things you're adamant about, such as body piercing and tattoos, you have to stand your ground. Do so for as long as you can, especially if the desire is based on peer pressure. As long as a child is living in your house, you should have influence over him. Once your child is independent, he'll make his own decisions. When it happens, you need to be supportive but remain clear about your position. For example, while our nephew lived with us and started college at seventeen, we didn't allow him to stay out all night at a friend's without calling us. When he moved into his own apartment, we still wanted to know if he would not be home. We would worry if we didn't hear from him. He knew our position, but we could not force the issue. Now, that he's twenty-two, when he's going out of town or won't be home for more than an overnight, he still lets us know—and we appreciate it.

You also want your child to be an independent thinker and not do things just because "everybody else is doing it." Before giving the nod for the hair streaks, ask her why she wants to do this. Help her to discern if she's really thought it through. If she still wants to do it, let her enjoy it. But if she decides that she hadn't given it enough thought and just got excited about the idea when the girls were all talking about it at lunch that day, and she now realizes she doesn't want to do it, acknowledge that decision. Tell her you're proud of her for thinking it through and making her own choices.

When it comes to fads, what often works best is self-disclosure. Talk about the things that were popular when you were a child and how few of them are around anymore (though that argument may not work if lava lamps and fluorescent stickers were all the rage when you were a child—since they're back). Remind him about the time he wanted every single Beanie Baby, then lost interest after he had spent so much of his allowance on them, only to discover there was a new fad. Help children to be realistic about what fads they can afford to participate in by encouraging them to save their money and buy the item on their own. But do keep in mind that not all fads are bad. The butterfly clips girls like to wear in their hair, for instance, are an inexpensive fad you may enjoy shopping for with your daughter. In this way, by sharing a harmless fad, you're also experiencing joy together.

Defining Positive Role Models

Role models can be a wonderful source of socialization for your children. They help your child form images of the kind of person he wants to become. They don't have to be big-name athletes or TV personalities. Anyone your child can identify with or respect and who behaves in constructive ways can be an effective role model. Of course, you can be your child's role model, but there may be others, such as an older student in the neighborhood or the older sibling of a friend, who:

1. Shares common interests.
2. Is available to offer support and guidance.
3. Inspires your child to follow through with goals.
4. Motivates your child to do his personal best.
5. Offers constructive feedback when your child is off track.

Positive peer and adult role models serve as guides. They can demonstrate through their own personal experiences and struggles how to cope with difficulties and exercise good judgment. This is especially important in facing adversity. Role models show that what matters is not that you have problems and temptations but how you deal with them. Making time for your children to visit and interact with positive people will help you in guiding and motivating them.

You may also want to spend time with them reading the biographies of successful people, like inventors, entertainers, political leaders or their favorite author. In those stories, your children will learn that along the road to success the people they admire had role models on whom *they* depended for support and guidance.

Living the Seventh Principle

Growing up among peers isn't easy for our children, but the alternative of never learning to handle the ups and downs of socialization will not adequately prepare them for a future in which they'll have co-workers, bosses, store clerks, and professionals with whom they must be able to communicate. In acknowledging the existence of peer pressure in your child's life and preparing him to deal with it, you are saying to your child:

- Think things through for yourself and don't follow others blindly.
- Take pride in yourself.
- Resist negative peer pressure.

- Remember the lessons Mom and Dad teach you.
- Communicate with us. We love you and are here for you.

By sharing these thoughts, you open the door for your child to grow into an emotionally secure adult with a sense of belonging, knowing that the family is there for support when it's needed.

8

Allow Time for Spirituality and Joy: The Eighth Principle

*I will allow time for joy each day, whether it
be a smile, a tickle, laughter, or play. Joy gives
my family the balance we need to function.
Our spirituality nourishes our love.*

Feeling the warmth of a tiny hand in your larger one, watching your child succeed at something that's important to her, listening to your children play together. These moments are just a trickle in the stream of spiritual and joyful experiences that you as a parent will be privileged to witness.

Yet if you don't make time in your family life for spirituality and joy, there will be a nagging sense of a void and emptiness. In this chapter we'll guide you toward allowing spirituality into your family life and toward improving the ways you may already do so. Then we'll discuss lighter matters, like making time for fun with your children and your partner.

Draw from Spirituality

Perhaps the experience of Emanuel Cleaver, former mayor of Kansas City, Missouri, will ring a bell for you. He wrote in an issue of *Daily Word* about really seeing something clearly that had before been so familiar. One day he called his wife and two children out into the backyard. He told them to walk with him to the end of the yard and turn around to look at their house surrounded by trees and the clouds above.

"I experienced goose bumps just looking. The wind was blowing gently as I looked at my family and said, 'We've been blessed to have this house and yard. Every person, place and thing that God has created is special because the presence of God is there. God is with us whether we live in a shanty or a big house, in the country or in the city,'" he wrote.

By sharing his joy in simple things with his family, this father was demonstrating spirituality and enduring values. He was creating a positive spiritual environment.

A positive spiritual environment established in moments of joy can be a source of great comfort and knowledge during stressful times. Spirituality enabled the late tennis great Arthur Ashe to impart a message of strength to his daughter Camera in the book *Days of Grace:* "Be ruled by that rule we call golden. Do unto others as you would have others do unto you. Do not beg God for favors. Instead, ask God for the wisdom to know what is right, what God wants done, and the will to do it."

Acknowledge Your Family's Spiritual Needs

All families face difficult times, from illness to financial hardship to the day-to-day stresses that we all must get through, but that can get to us just the same. What do you rely on to get you through? When it comes to your children's morals and values, what will be the source of their beliefs?

No matter what religion you are or how often you worship, the religious precepts you were raised with are likely to surface when you need them most. But what about your children? What belief system are you teaching them? What spiritual life have you given them to draw upon? In a time in which the material world offers promises of ultimate satisfaction if only you purchase the latest noisy, flashy item on your TV screen, are you trying to offer an alternative?

If you believe that a child enters the world with a loving, open soul, your responsibility as a parent is to fulfill the role of spiritual nurturer. This is not easy, given several factors:

- You may still be trying to resolve your own conflicts. A lifetime of spiritual growth within yourself means that you have not reached the point where growing and searching have ended. With your children you are being asked to impart what you're not completely sure of or comfortable with yourself.

- Life consists of one busy day after another, and it's not unusual to feel that "the faster I go, the behinder I get." God and spirituality may not seem as urgent as work responsibilities, household needs, and other family concerns.

- You may be a single parent because of death, divorce, or choice. No matter how spiritual you are, you will still deal with sorrow, anger, or other disturbing and distracting feelings.

- You may have to rely on outside child care, further reducing the time spent with your children.

- You may be searching for something beyond yourself and beyond what you know as fact. Questioning your relationship to others, to your surroundings, to the world/universe in which you live, you may find that your mind, heart, and soul are filled with more questions than answers.

But even with these challenges, it's a parent's responsibility to make every effort to foster and encourage spirituality in children. A strong connection to the spirit gives children an enormous advantage as they strive to be psychologically and emotionally healthy people.

Stu and JoAnne put their children first and continued to worship together even though they were divorced. They worked together to plan their son's bar mitzvah. The ceremony was somewhat complicated because they had to decide how to involve each other's new spouses and their new stepchildren. They wanted to be sensitive to everyone's feelings while being clear that their son's best interests came first. They were successful, and their efforts will be something their son will remember as he grows older, even if he doesn't fully understand it now.

"Mixed" Partnerships

Your family's spiritual quest could be complicated if you're not on the same page when it comes to religion and spirituality. While it's true that worshipping together and having similar beliefs can be a big part of the foundation for strong relationships, some families are successful even when this ingredient isn't included. For example, Marcia and Stan are dealing with this.

Marcia's a Catholic, and Stan's a Baptist. They worship at different churches but share common values. Although their children go to a Catholic school and mass on Sunday, they also periodically worship at Stan's church.

Janet is Jewish, and Ben is Christian. They've been married for fifteen years and have raised their children with an understanding of both religions. They, like many couples, successfully share different religious perspectives with their children.

As you can imagine in today's diverse society, there are any number of combinations of religious beliefs: Each parent follows a different religion, one parent is actively religious but the other is not, levels of belief in God vary, and so on. The success of such "mixed" partnerships can well depend on the two people involved arriving at an understanding and accommodation with each other. Beyond that, an essential part of parenting together is having and acting upon an understanding with each other of how to raise children when beliefs, levels of belief, or practices are different and sometimes even oppositional.

We want to emphasize that although up to this point we've spoken about the benefits of belief in God, incorporating that in child rearing and nurturing the soul and spirituality of children, we're not saying that being an agnostic or atheist means you're doomed to be a poor parent or that your children can't grow up with psychological and emotional health. We do think, though, that not having a connection to God robs a person and a parent of a powerful source of strength. The key is not whom you call "god" but that there is respect and reverence for a more powerful force in your life that you want to share with your child. We are Christian and share our beliefs and love of the Lord with our children. However, we respect others' beliefs and religions.

So when we talk about the mixed partnership, we're referring to parents who may have differing views, practices, levels of interest, and/or questions. But you are nonetheless committed to helping your children acknowledge the presence of a higher power or, at the very least, that an exploration of the varied aspects of spirituality is a worthwhile and lifelong activity.

If you're in a mixed relationship, here are some suggestions as to how you and your partner can work together to nurture and make use of spirituality in raising your children:

1. *Talk to each other about what God means to you.*

2. *Agree to ways you can express faith as a team on occasion by worshipping or praying together.*

3. *Use prayer to defuse conflicts.* Stop, pray silently, then pray together.

4. *Seek and ask forgiveness when you make a mistake.*

5. *Admit that you have faults, make mistakes, can be defensive, express negativity.* You may not choose to go into detail, especially if you're no longer with your child's other parent, but at least admit that you're not perfect.

6. *If you are a believer, invite the Holy Spirit in to help express love, whether you're a couple or not.* Demonstrating the love of God in your interactions is affirming and self-enhancing.

7. *Don't equate a lack of interest in a specific religion as a lack of spirituality.* Your partner may still be very involved in searching for answers and in nurturing spirituality in your children without having committed to a specific belief system.

Ten Ways to Teach Your Children about Faith

Parents sometimes wonder how and when you can teach children about God's place in your lives. The answer depends on what you already do. You may have attended a worship service the first scheduled day after you brought your child home from the hospital. Perhaps your children are being raised in a church, synagogue, or other house of worship. Or maybe you attend only on religious holidays or periodically.

It's best to teach children about God in proactive and reactive ways. Being proactive involves attending services, praise, worship, reading the Bible, etc. Reactive parenting means discussing life's challenges and relying on faith and prayer and teaching children to rely on spiritual strengths to deal with problem situations. It's best to begin this process as early as possible in developmentally appropriate ways. Songs, children's prayers, and books are the beginning methods. As children develop, they start to ask questions and are able to discuss faith and beliefs more openly.

Here are some questions that will help you evaluate to what extent God is a presence in your relationship with your partner and with your children. There are no right or wrong answers. However, the answers, as we discuss them, will either reinforce what you already do with your children or inspire positive change.

The first five questions are from parent to parent:

1. *Do you talk to each other about God?*

    Talking about God allows you to open up about your deepest wishes and desires, particularly for your children. Talk about how you grew up and what religion and spirituality meant to you.

2. *Do you pray, attend services, or in other ways worship together?*

    These can be bonding experiences that provide opportunities for fellowship and understanding. Praying together reveals your soul's passion and allows your divine purpose to unfold. It's a way to communicate beyond the everyday conversations and exchanges—it's deeper and more meaningful.

3. *Do you connect your faith to everyday life practices with your partner?*

    It's easier to pray for peace, love, and understanding than to demonstrate it during difficult times. Parents need to show how their beliefs and values can positively affect everyday life. Couples need to connect with God during an argument or stressful situation in order to then connect with each other and attempt to resolve the situation in a productive manner, with a loving spirit.

4. *Do you openly ask for and offer forgiveness when needed from your partner?*

    Seeking and offering forgiveness can be a humbling experience, very difficult to do, but it's also empowering. When you assume responsibility for your own actions, you have a greater opportunity for self-growth and development.

5. *Do you actively teach religious principles to your children?*

Even if it's saying grace or a bedtime prayer, it's comforting and affirming for children to see that their parents share practices, even if they're not living together. Depending on the degree of unresolved issues between parents, sharing some form of religious practice together provides a sense of security and stability for children.

Boundaries need to be clear, so that children don't get confused or experience heightened fantasies about reconciliation between you and your former partner. You need to handle each situation in age-appropriate ways. For example, a Christian mother with a thirteen-year-old son could say, "Daddy and I still care about each other, and we both love God very much. We will never be married again. We don't love each other in that way anymore, but we do love each other as brother and sister in Christ."

Now, from parent to child:

6. *Do you talk to each other about God?*

Letting your children know your beliefs and views helps them to form a foundation and understanding of God. It's fine to be open about your struggles and questions. This can happen particularly when a loved one dies or there's a crisis. Allow your children to experience your joys and sorrows in age-appropriate ways. You wouldn't go into as much detail with a five-year-old as you would with a fifteen-year-old. With a five-year-old you might say, "My Uncle Duckett died, and I'm very sad. I'm praying to God. I believe that Uncle Duckett is in heaven, and I'm glad he isn't in pain anymore, but I will miss him." To a fifteen-year-old you may say, "I'm praying to God for strength and understanding. Sometimes it's hard to understand why things happen. I wanted Uncle Duckett to heal and get better, but I have to accept that it was not God's will. Sometimes I feel angry and confused, but I pray to God for peace. I'm glad that he isn't suffering any longer. Yet I miss him."

It's just as important to listen to your children's thoughts, feelings, and beliefs, particularly as situations arise in which they might question their faith and have doubts.

7. *Do your children participate in religious training?*

Hebrew school, Sunday school, and other formalized ways of teaching children about their religion clearly provide added values and morals. They allow children to learn and apply religious teachings. Children can share information with parents and further develop a spiritual bond.

8. *Do you pray, attend services, or in other ways worship together?*

Doing so allows you to bond further and share emotions on a deeper level. It offers children stability, discipline, and structure. Parents can guide their children's view of God and help them to avoid seeing God as punitive and judgmental.

9. *Do you openly ask for and express forgiveness with your children?*

Asking forgiveness from children can be difficult for parents, but it can also be one of the best bonding experiences between parent and child. Children need to know that parents aren't perfect and make mistakes, too. Some parents fear that to admit a mistake will diminish their power and authority. But quite the opposite is true. Instead, it provides for greater communication, compassion, and understanding.

10. *Do you make/recognize a connection between your interaction with your children and your belief in and worship of God?*

Children learn from what you do more than from what you say. They need to see you demonstrate your faith in everyday interactions, whether it's showing forgiveness toward your partner or a friend for a trespass against you or showing kindness to a stranger. Children need to know that you put God first in your life by making sacrifices to do what is right even when you want to do something that seems good but is not good for you.

For example, you may be sorely tempted to offer a rather unfriendly gesture to the driver who just cut you off. It would feel good for a few moments, and you would let him know what you thought of his behavior. But is it worth it? What message are you sending your child, who just witnessed the exchange? "What would Jesus do?" is what we can think instead.

At the same time, when you fail, don't beat yourself up. In fact, you can say to your child, "I just lost it with that person. What he did was wrong, but I'm disappointed in the way I handled it. I'm sorry I did it and even more sorry that it wasn't a good example for you."

Simple Spiritual Messages for Children

Signs of affection, respect, excitement, happiness, and love are life-affirming examples for your children, whether you practice a religion or not.

Even the smallest spiritual act can make a big impression on children. Recall how Mr. Cleaver wanted to share his experience with his family. Your religion offers many rituals and practices you can utilize with your children, or go ahead and develop your own. What's most important is the act of creating and sharing time or events that strengthen a spiritual bond. Here are some more recommendations:

- Say "I love you" at least once a day to acknowledge your blessing and appreciation of your family. This also includes physical affection—a kiss, a hug, a warm stroke on the back.

- Do inspirational reading together that highlights struggles and triumphs in life.

- Attend plays, musicals, and other cultural events that have a spiritual base or message.

- Perform a good deed together. Working on a fund drive for a local charity, visiting a nursing home, donating toys or books to a hospital, bringing food and clothing to a local food pantry—all these are simple yet much-appreciated acts that strengthen your family's spiritual connection, as well as your child's connection to the world.

- Find unique and "fun" ways to communicate with each other. Leave notes for each other containing positive, affectionate thoughts or e-mail messages from work. These are things that can even be done by parents who no longer live with their child.

Simple Religious Messages for Children

We advocate family involvement in the worship of God. The positive attributes of spirituality are closely connected to God's gifts, which have been bestowed on us and are available every day. Children who are instructed in God's goodness and grow up having faith in and love for our Creator have an enormous foundation upon which they can form and maintain spiritually satisfying lives.

For many people, worship of God combines practices and sharing of beliefs at home and participation in a church, temple, or mosque. A place of worship can be a nurturing, life-empowering environment and a lifelong foundation of support. But you may not like to attend services and prefer to worship God in your own way. For you, your relationship with God is more personal and solitary. What's important is that you recognize the intimate link to God that spirituality provides and impress this upon your children.

Parents can team up to offer messages to children that introduce them to the presence of God in their lives, as well as to the whole concept of spirituality. Of course, children should receive different messages at different ages.

For the preschooler, you can say:

- God loves you.
- God forgives you.
- God wants what is best for you.
- God wants you to be happy.
- Pray and tell God what you think and feel. Always tell God the truth and you will tell yourself the truth.

For the grade-schooler, you can add:

- God's grace gives you the opportunity to fulfill any dream.
- Pray for God's will in all things.
- Be still at times and experience the peace of God.
- Discipline, responsibility, and order help you focus on God. Learn to do something consistently and on schedule. Rituals can be helpful.
- Overcoming fear is trusting God.

For adolescents, try adding:

- God doesn't punish you. You punish yourself with guilt, fear, and shame. Avoid doing things that lead to those feelings. But if you don't, forgive yourself.
- There is divine order, and God has a divine purpose for you.
- Your life reflects your conscious and subconscious choices. Stay aware and centered in God.
- Do what is pleasing in God's sight.
- God gave us free will. Learn to be disciplined in your choices.

These are guides for discussion for believing families. The goal is to have open dialogue and share your beliefs with your children. Modify them, add to them, and respond to your child's questions.

Simple Fun

Most families look forward to vacations to focus fully on joy. However, joy can be experienced in many ways on a daily basis. A spontaneous hug, a belly laugh, a dance from the "olden days" performed to celebrate a good report card are ways in which the bonded family looks out for and supports each other. (A friend of ours, Winston Johnson, is director of social work services for Hartford Public Schools in Connecticut. Both of his children are honor students. This gives him a great deal of exercise, because for every A they receive, Winston does a little jig, dancing around the house.)

Our friends Milton and Sandra Maxwell are our son's godparents. A couple of summers ago they came to visit. Their two adult daughters, Plesetta and Lakeista, also came. Plesetta is married and has a young son, Collin, who came, too. The bond between the family members is so strong and inspiring. They allow time for joy and respect each other's differences. Watching them share stories and exchange loving glances taught us to appreciate each other more. They enjoy spending time together, and although they have their individual interests and lives, they make time to enhance their bond. They take family vacations together, and they go out to dinner, shopping, community events, church, movies, and plays together.

Our friend Pam is another model for our family. Godmother to our son, she helps coordinate many of our family parties and gatherings. She is divorced from the two fathers of her five adult children. However, over the years and still now when she has a celebration, both of her ex-husbands attend. The two fathers support and guide all of her children, even the ones who are not their biological children. They support each other, laugh, and nurture one another. Pam's ex-husbands are still bonded as a family unit. Their new partners understand the dynamic after spending a few minutes in Pam's company. She is warm, caring, and compassionate and knows how to experience joy. Pam will often plan family functions that include lots of cheer and fun. Clearly, whatever issues led to the divorces, all members understand the importance of maintaining a bond with the children.

But this didn't just happen for the Maxwells or Pam's family, and it won't just happen for you. Take this inventory to find out where to begin.

1. Do you laugh together often as a family?

2. Do you organize a family outing at least once a month?

3. Do you act silly with your family at times?

4. Do you vacation together as a family?

5. Do you set aside a day together without the distraction of work or other commitments?

6. Do you ask your children what fun activities they would like to participate in?

7. Do you experience fun times with extended family members?

8. Do you find ways to experience spiritual peace and joy, like taking the time to help others?

9. Do you express affection and verbalize the joy of bonding?

10. Do you engage in established loving behaviors, such as group family hugs or using sign language to say "I love you"?

If you answered no to any of these questions, you can probably get to yes with just a little effort and attention.

If you answered no to many or most, there are probably underlying issues that negatively affect your family's ability to experience joy. There are likely to be issues that relate to one or more of the previous principles. For example, family communication might be poor, or siblings might be too hostile toward each other to enjoy interacting, or your adolescent might consistently prefer to be with peers. Addressing these principles will lead to greater opportunities to experience joy.

Develop a personal action plan of how you will focus on the deficit areas.

1. Buy a children's joke book and share jokes as a family one night after dinner.

2. Have each member suggest and coordinate (children with assistance) an outing.

3. Do something out of character. Act silly, dress up like it's Halloween, dance around the house, and so on.

4. Start a savings plan for the vacation. It doesn't necessarily take a great deal of money to have a vacation. Yes, certainly some can be expensive. However, a drive to visit relatives in another state can be structured like a vacation.

5. Coordinate a family play date. This could be an outing or a day of playing board games or watching a good video as a family.

6. Join one of your children's activities. Let them choose what they want to "take" you to do, for example, the zoo, a movie, skating.

7. Visit extended family or consider a family reunion.

8. Along with your child, volunteer or spend time at a nursing home, adopt a family for the holidays, or be a mentor.

9. Say "I love you" often and give lots of hugs. Find other ways to express affection and love.

What's the Rush? Slow Down

As important as your extended family, friends, community members, child's school, and your work all are to your family, you also need time just to be your individual unit. Families need time alone first and foremost to get to know each other on a deeper and more meaningful level. Many of us are rushing from task to task and activity to activity. Sometimes it's best just to relax and have quiet time together when nothing is structured or scheduled. This allows for freedom of expression and spontaneous interactions.

You may find it difficult to allow this unstructured time to occur in your family. There's always one more thing that needs to be done before you can sit and read a story to your child, one more errand to run before you can go to the park. It happens to all of us. But think about the unexpected days that you have to stay home from work because your child is sick or the snow day that keeps you all home. Suddenly your routine for the day is thrown awry. Instead of focusing on the planned tasks of the day, why not go with the flow? Some of your family's greatest joy will come from the spontaneous actions you allow when you just live in the moment. A child's sick day can be a time to snuggle and pull out family photo albums, so you can talk about his life and show him how he's grown. A snow day can turn into a friendly snowball fight on the front lawn, followed by hot chocolate and a board game while you all wear pajamas and fuzzy slippers.

But don't wait until these unexpected moments occur. You can create opportunities for quality time every day, even when doing chores. Finding the joy in the most mundane tasks can be exhilarating. For instance, a grocery store trip with the whole family may seem daunting, but it can be fun, too, as you assign each member items on the list to find, everyone choosing the best prices and brands and helping unload the cart and bag the groceries. This becomes a good learning experience for your children in many ways, not the least of which is to become savvy consumers.

And children love to help their parents. You can model having a good time doing chores. In our household when we clean, we turn on the music, taking breaks to dance or sing and praise each other as we move along.

You can also make sure you set aside a time each week that's "just for family" time, with no community, work, or school commitments allowed—unless that's part of your joint family activity. It can mean a Friday-night video and a pizza, a Saturday-night game night, or a Sunday-morning walk in the park with the family dog. When possible, strive to eat dinner together every night, so you can share your thoughts and experiences about your day. In fact, studies show that family meals help teenagers in particular deal with the pressures of adolescence, most likely because they have the chance to communicate with their parents and be heard. You can also set aside time each night to read to your children—no matter how well they read on their own. As any teacher will tell you, children—even the older "child"—love to be read to.

But don't plan all this quality time on your own. Get your child's input. As parents, part of your joy comes from watching your children have fun and enjoy life. You want them to have a "happy childhood," but sometimes you may forget to include them in determining what that looks like. Asking your child's advice and input into ways to set aside family time can be very enlightening. Children will gladly let you know what they need and want to do to have fun.

And children have great ideas. A picnic, walking in the rain together, camping out in the backyard, building a tent in a bedroom to sleep in, having a popcorn fight, reading scary stories, going hiking, going bike riding, and so on. There's an endless list of things that children will tell you are fun for them.

Set Aside Parent Time

But as wonderful as it is to set aside time with your children, parents also need time for themselves and for each other. You need to be able to regroup. You need time to assess how things are going and to devise a "strategic plan" for further growth and improvement. All couples can easily become overwhelmed and overextended and forget to check in with one another. Couple-bonding time allows for greater bonded family time.

When you fail to save time for yourselves, despite your best intentions for your family, you and your children are affected. You may lose sight of your friendship and romance with your partner, which leads to feelings of frustration, resentment, and an emotional void.

Children "feel" the effects in their parents' interaction with them. Sometimes you're unaware of your irritability or preoccupation. Your marriage can become boring or stagnant, which at the extreme could lead to infidelity or emotional distancing. Couples who have fun together—whether that means going out dancing, to dinner, playing Scrabble, or taking a bubble bath together—share feelings of emotional intimacy and closeness. Children sense and experience their parents' emotional connection—and thrive on it.

Remember back to the first three Principles. Before you were parents, you were individuals who came together with your past intact and together formed a new life. That relationship cannot be forgotten. If you feel as though you're not communicating as well as you would like, revisit Principle Three to determine what, if any, old communication patterns you may be falling back into.

Couples need time to strengthen their friendship and love relationship. When two people are feeling valued and cherished by each other, this leads to feelings of satisfaction, joy, and fulfillment. You're then more capable of allowing time for joy with your children. Setting aside time for dates and making love increases your ability to experience pleasure in other areas of our life. It also helps reduce your stress, allowing you to be more productive and efficient.

Just as you were innovative about making time for your children, make time for each other. Maybe Friday night after the children go to bed can be your time to have a cup of coffee or glass of wine and just sit and talk about your week. Make a "phone date" each day to check in on each other, even if it's for a brief chat. Send each other e-mails from work if it's not against company policy. Include notes in each other's briefcases. You probably have noticed by now that the very things you do for your children to let them know they're important to you are the same things you can do for your partner.

And just as you want to set aside chore-free time for your children, you want to set aside work-free time for your partner. But that's not a hard-and-fast rule if the work you have is shared. Perhaps you're painting the living room together. Put on music and whistle while you work. When Jackie and Brett had to send out holiday cards, instead of Jackie doing it by herself as she so often did, she and Brett made a date of it, complete with a roaring fire in the fireplace, holiday music, and mulled cider. Just as must-do tasks with your children can be fun, so, too can those shared with your partner.

Laugh together, reminisce, and take the time to show your affection for one another. Not only will you feel more connected as teammates in parenting, you'll also be modeling for your children what loving relationships look like.

Of course, every parent knows that whenever children are awake, they're always willing to interrupt any intimate moment or conversation you and your partner share. When children interrupt, you should remind them to say "excuse me." If you're engaged in a conversation that you don't want interrupted, say, "Mommy and I are talking right now. Please give us a few minutes, and then we'll give you our attention." But when you can, you may want to pause a moment and listen to your child, then return to your conversation. Your willingness to let your conversation be interrupted will depend on the timing and depth of the discussion.

The Value of Family Meetings

Jed and Nelda didn't understand why their fourteen-year-old daughter, Deidre, was always hostile and angry toward their eighteen-year-old son, Paul. The tension had been building over the years. Finally, one day when her mother was chastising her for being so negative toward her brother, Deidre, in a fit of rage, disclosed that Paul had molested her from the time she was nine to twelve years old. On several occasions at night while she was asleep, he would put his hand down her panties. Deidre would awake feeling angry, confused, and violated but never told on her brother because of feelings of guilt, shame, and embarrassment.

At first Paul denied it, but then he broke down in tears and showed genuine remorse. In treatment, the family had to heal from the wounds of betrayal, pain, hurt, and anger.

This is an extreme case, but the dynamic of unresolved feelings of hurt and harboring secrets of painful experiences is common in many families. For example:

Anita felt that her mother showed preferential treatment toward her brother. More responsibility was placed on her for household responsibilities, and her brother was doted on. This was a constant source of tension in the family.

Ervin felt that his father favored his brother Earl because Earl was a better athlete.

Courtney felt that her mother loved her sister more because she was the "pretty" one.

Unless everyone has a forum in which to air grievances, the hostilities felt by family members will grow to the point where they can no longer be ignored. At that point families will be caught in a vicious cycle of bad will toward one another rather than joy.

While all families will experience hostilities, on the overall scale, the joy should far outweigh the unhappiness if everyone has a chance to be heard and understood. This doesn't mean that everyone has to agree, but there should be ongoing dialogue.

Sometimes there's a person who acts as the "switchboard" in the family. Everyone conveys information to this person, and he or she communicates it to the rest of the family. This is harmful. Often information is changed or censored when communicated through another person. The intent of the message will become distorted or modified and its original meaning lost. To change this pattern, the person who needs to communicate must be encouraged and supported in speaking directly to the particular person with whom he or she has a grievance.

Together, take another look at the Seven Golden Rules of Communication. Remember to:

1. Initiate dialogue.

2. Listen actively.

3. Validate feelings.

4. Wait your turn.

5. Stay on the subject.

6. Fight fair.

7. Respect differences.

Focus on active listening to address grievances in your family. Each person who has a grievance should get the "floor" to voice his or her concerns. The other members should then paraphrase or restate what was said.

Try starting the meetings with a prayer and ending with a prayer that focuses on increased understanding in the future.

Learn to Manage Anger Together

Your family's communication also depends on how you deal with anger together. Anger is one of the most difficult emotions to manage. Your first impulse when expressing it will be to lash out or respond aggressively. Practicing the art of assertive communication requires commitment and practice.

Dealing with anger requires learning ways to defuse tension, stress, and explosive incidents. Anger is a normal emotion, but family members have to learn ways to express it that don't hurt or destroy relationships. Common techniques include:

- Counting to ten while slowly inhaling and exhaling a deep breath or two before you speak.
- Taking a time-out.
- Stopping and asking God to help the communication to go more smoothly. "Inviting God in" helps to initiate a calming influence and an attitude of "peacemaking."
- Remember the "I feel angry because . . ." statement, instead of the accusatory "You made me angry . . ." "You shouldn't have . . ."

Celebrations and Reunions: The Power of Making Memories Together

As you develop traditions and rituals in which you share family values, your values come alive. For example, if your child has successfully completed a goal, a family celebration will add to her memories of being important and worthy to the family, as well as to the family legacy.

Many families share stories and experiences of past generations and ancestors at family reunions. Derek's grandmother coordinated a yearly family reunion picnic. Cars would be lined up for an entire block. This event showed the family members ways to enjoy being close and connected and gave everyone a sense of belonging and a responsibility to continue the tradition.

The family reunion picnics continued for many years after the death of Derek's grandmother and developed into family barbecues at his mother's or uncle's beautiful home, far from the early picnics that were held at the local park near Elizabeth, New Jersey. Although they have become more elaborate and all who attend experience joy, simple pleasures remain from the past. There are great memories from the days when Derek's grandmother was alive, and we cherish her legacy.

Darlene's family has a very similar history and tradition. Her parents take our children to her father's extended-family reunion every two years. These reunions include people from all over the country and involve a weekend of festivities, including talent shows, guest speakers, a banquet, and many other activities.

Not only do your children need to understand their place in your family, they also need to understand their place in the world. They need a sense of belonging and a connection to their heritage. You can help them achieve this by allowing them the opportunity to make their own memories with the people in your lives.

When Dotteanna and Derek Jr. attend family gatherings, they're nurtured and supported in ways that we can't provide. Eating their grandmother's Thanksgiving dressing and playing basketball with their grandfather in the backyard are memories that give them a sense of security and position. They know that they're loved and valued by many people, and this gives them a greater sense of self-efficacy and confidence of their place in the world. For your children, this sense of connection can come from the people in your church, your neighborhood, the friend who is almost like a sister to you, as well as from your parents.

Family projects are another means of celebrating your team spirit. As a family, for example, you can organize activities that enable you to give back some of the blessings you've received. Taking the time to visit the elderly or donating clothes and toys to needy children gives your entire family a sense of joy that receiving could never give. Helping others helps create a sense of purpose and fulfillment of God's plan for us. We feel divinely guided and truly blessed.

You might consider scheduling regular community projects for your family—which you can then all discuss and vote on—such as working in a soup kitchen on Thanksgiving, organizing a park cleanup in the spring, or collecting canned goods for a local pantry. When children see themselves as part of a larger picture by working alongside you, they learn the value of living your spirituality and feel the joy that comes from being part of something bigger than themselves. In our materialistic society this is one of the greatest gifts that team-spirited parenting can give your children.

Living the Eighth Principle

When you laugh and play with one another and give and share of your time and selves, you will release feelings of spirituality and joy. These feelings will help your family grow as a loving team.

Of course, things can go wrong in families, from the accidental, hurtful comment, to the more pervasive behaviors that can lead to separation and divorce for parents and disconnection from your child. That's why forgiveness in families is as critical as communication. You'll certainly make mistakes and inevitably hurt one another. How you move beyond these experiences will determine the strength of your family's bond and ability to experience joy.

Forgiveness is as powerful an action for the injured party as it is for the offender. When you have a forgiving spirit, you open yourself up to be able to experience joy fully. Harboring feelings of resentment or anger interferes with this process. It also sends a negative message to your children that their mistakes will not be forgiven. Eventually they may stop trying. Your child needs to know that she can learn from mistakes and that although you may be disappointed or angry, she's always loved.

Nurture your children in the spirit of joy, and expect them to become strong, healthy branches of your family tree.

Index

Printed in the USA
CPSIA information can be obtained
at www.ICGtesting.com
JSHW082159140824
68134JS00014B/318